threeS into Infinity

Sarah Elizabeth Moreman

BookLeaf
Publishing

India | USA | UK

Presentation by *BookLeaf Publishing*

Web: www.bookleafpub.com

E-mail: info@bookleafpub.com

ISBN: 9789363310780

First edition 2024

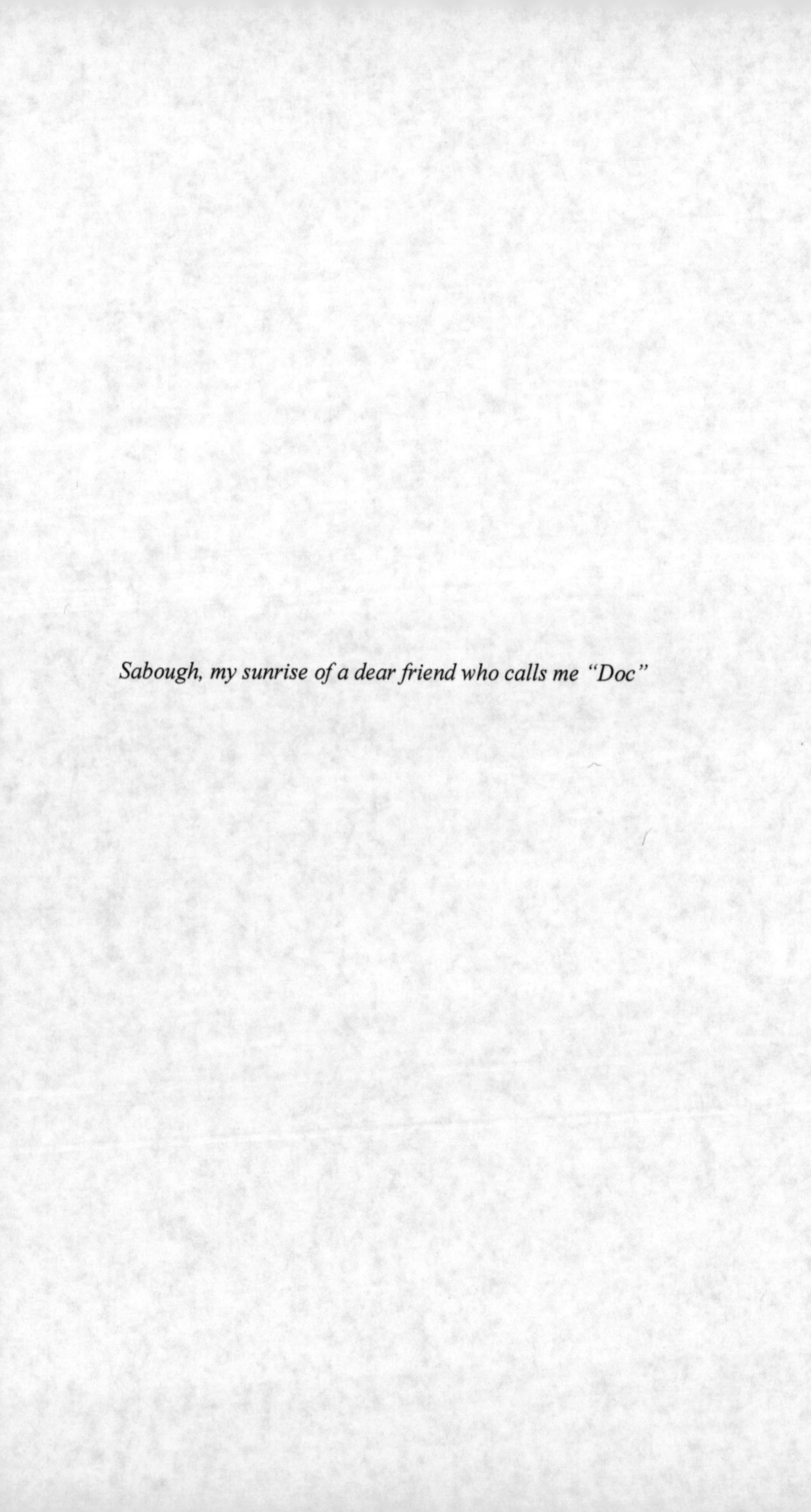

Sabough, my sunrise of a dear friend who calls me "Doc"

ACKNOWLEDGEMENT

The Sonrise of my life, Whose hem I hold onto for dignity, integrity, patience, understanding, and peace.

To my parents who did not take the well-grooved path of raising their baby who was born with a profound bilateral sensorineural hearing loss. Instead, they chose for me to make the decision on my own, including cochlear implantation.

My fierce friend advocating for me to take my Ferrari out for a spin, Jane Wheat Bruce and her sister, my 11th grade transliterator and Chemistry aficionado, Ginger Wheat Key.

My soul sister always, Bethany Irene Lundell Garver and her sister, my Córdoba-experienced, hiking friend, Joan Marie Lundell.

My blonde warrioress, Deborah Strawn, who has seen me through each chapter of my life, especially in the area of education.

MED-EL cochlear implant surgery team – Dr. Amy Munning Arthur, Dr. Stephanie Axtell, and Dr. Dennis G. Pappas, Jr.

Gracias por el curso intensivo de español con margaritas para prepararme para mi viaje a Córdoba, Argentina – Julie McCormick Veal.

For being my Activation Day support team – my parents, Grammy, sister Josie Moreman Stamps, nephew Jack Stamps, niece Claire Stamps, lastborn nephew Charles "Mr. Happy" Stamps, Aunt Glen Bradley Jones, Aunt Beth Bradley Landreth, MyBaby Kate Daisy Petty with her baby son Jett, cousins Greg & Dede Wood, Deborah Strawn, Jane Bruce, Beverly Linam Kennedy, Jennifer Alverson, Ryan Nelson, Efosa Anthony Oni, Robyn Braxton Booth, and Krystal Ann "Pino" Leeds.

My LIV Parkside traveling sister, mother of Miss Grace, hostess for Córdoba, Argentina and CDMX destinations, Nomad Tax boss, and my bridesmaid to her bride, Krystal Ann "Pino" Leeds.

TEDxBirmingham – connector Gabriel Tajeu, speaker coach Anne Wright Rygiel, organizer Matthew Hamilton, co-organizer Rebecca Dobrinski, Suzan Summers Brandt.

Close friends who made the decision to take the plunge long before I did – Leslie Mossholder Patout, Lucy Mossholder Lowe, Bethani Ford Smith, Ryan Hickman, and Christina Liu Konsko.

Photography credits
Front cover photo by
Heather Newman of Newman's Photography
Lower Alabama

Back cover photo by
Diana Johnson of J'adore Boudoir Studio – Diana Johnson Photography
Birmingham, Alabama

PREFACE

MED-EL description of a cochlear implant

Cochlear implants are designed for people with severe to profound sensorineural hearing loss. With this type of hearing loss, the hair cells in the inner ear are damaged and can't detect sounds properly. A cochlear implant bypasses these damaged hair cells and sends electric signals to the brain, where they are interpreted as sound.

A cochlear implant system has two main components. The externally worn audio processor detects sounds and sends them to the internal implant, which is placed just under the skin behind the ear.

– MED-EL, *the author's choice for a cochlear implant*

Website | https://www.medel.com/en-us

What is a cochlear implant?

Cochlear implants are small electronic devices that allow people to hear sounds. A cochlear implant does not restore normal hearing, but it can help people to understand speech with less reliance on lip reading and to perceive sounds.

A cochlear implant has two main parts:

♦ One part is outside of the ear. It has a microphone to detect sound, a battery to power the system, a processor to process sound, and a transmitter to send the electric signals to the internal part.
♦ The cochlear implant's internal part is implanted under the skin, with electrodes (wires) that extend into the cochlea (a structure in the inner ear). The electrodes respond to sound information captured by the outer processor and stimulate the neurons in the cochlea to create a signal that is picked up by the brain.

Cochlear Implant versus Hearing Aid

A cochlear implant is different than a hearing aid. Hearing aids make sounds louder but rely on the ear's natural hearing ability, so they may not work well for people with severe hearing loss due to damage in the inner ear (sensorineural hearing loss).

Cochlear implants directly stimulate the part of the ear that doesn't work by using a mild electrical current applied to the structures in the cochlea. A cochlear implant can help adults and children with severe hearing loss who cannot understand speech even with powerful hearing aids.

– Stephen Bowditch, AuD, MS, Johns Hopkins Medicine

Source
https://www.hopkinsmedicine.org/health/treatment-tests-and-therapies/cochlear-implants

---

NIDCD description of a cochlear implant

A cochlear implant is a small, complex electronic device that can help to provide a sense of sound to a person who is profoundly deaf or severely hard-of-hearing. The implant consists of an external portion that sits behind the ear and a second portion that is surgically placed under the skin. An implant has the following parts:

♦ A microphone, which picks up sound from the environment

♦ A speech processor, which selects and arranges sounds picked up by the microphone

♦ A transmitter and receiver/stimulator, which receive signals from the speech processor and convert them into electric impulses

♦ An electrode array, which is a group of electrodes that collects the impulses from the stimulator and sends them to different regions of the auditory nerve

An implant does not restore normal hearing. Instead, it can give a deaf person a useful representation of sounds in the environment and help him or her to understand speech.

How does a cochlear implant work?

A cochlear implant is very different from a hearing aid. Hearing aids amplify sounds so they may be detected by damaged ears. Cochlear implants bypass damaged portions of the ear and directly stimulate the auditory nerve. Signals generated by the implant are sent by way of the auditory nerve to the brain, which recognizes the signals as sound. Hearing through a cochlear implant is different from normal hearing and takes time to learn or relearn. However, it allows many people to recognize warning signals, understand other sounds in the environment, and understand speech in person or over the telephone.

– National Institute on Deafness and Other Communication Disorders (13 June 2024)

Source https://www.nidcd.nih.gov/health/cochlear-implants

Sss....arah, Sss-arah

Sensation of a breeze tiptoeing
across the back of my hair,
escaping the unexpected,
I turn to see faces ducking
behind hands and arms
shaking in laughter.
Across the room, Mrs. Wallwork
shakes her head, a scolding expression, lips thin
in disapproval at them.

Sssixth grade shenanigans

I frown in confusion, turning back
to the complicated math problem on paper,
a pencil gripped in my fingers, pressure
turning the tips white

I hold my breath, waiting
shoulders not moving, yet muscles hardening
in tension, waiting

Letting out my breath to relieve the hardness
as I lift a hand to smooth down my hair
back in place before focusing on the x
in the equation on paper

The *x* in the equation solved
years later, in the living room of Mrs. Wallwork,
Dee visiting and taking me up
that steep driveway where white walls reign

"They were whispering your name," she said.

Sss....arah, Sss-arah

The *Sss* breezily lifting my hair,
Raising my awareness of being different
Raising my awareness of being too trusting

The *x* in the equation solved

The *Sss* that my father wanted
Slushiness in my *Sss* for thirty-seven years
Now corrected
The *x* in the equation solved
Through surgery

Seventeen

Seventeen, the age of awareness
Seventeen, the age when my feline daughter
passed away, at the same time my wisdom
teeth were pulled, my cheeks puffed

Blood seeping through my cracked lips
Blood seeping from my grieving heart

Seventeen, the age of awareness
Seventeen, the age of adjustment
Seventeen, the age of letting go

What to let go?
    Convictions

Why? Death of a loved one, even a cat, can
bring into perspective that nothing stays

    Change is inevitable.

How do we let go of our built-in convictions?

Seventeen, the age of awareness
Seventeen, the age of learning about possibilities
The possibilities of changing

A visit from a friend from the town
of the other school,
she has embraced those possibilities,
She has changed.

      I watched her.

Holding the strange device in her hand
Yet the vacant expression associated
with the deaf still coats her face.

Other than the surgery, I do not see any change.
She was still responsive in a deaf way.

Seventeen and still holding onto my *convictions*.

Twenty-three

I am fine with the way I am.
	Why change?

I do receive sounds, albeit not
as perfectly as others, but I do
receive sounds.

Enough that I can tell the difference between
a male voice and a female voice.

I can hear the melody, the piano, the drums
in the music, simply not the lyrics, the words.

The words that I cannot decipher,
yet I dance in a way that others watch.

I am fine with the way I am.
	Why change?

Irritation waits to rise
whenever someone suggests that I change.

	Why change?
Why not accept me the way I am?

The supposed love and concern from him
as he tries to persuade me,

My eyes fierce as I sharply say no.
He tries to reason with me,
to take advantage of my father's position
in the military

The mistake of my telling him what my father
said, that his military insurance would cover
everything for me to hear more, to hear better
standard-wise.

How could I change what God has designed?
          I am perfectly fine with the way I am.

I communicate.
I speak.
I dance.

Anger and irritation rise as I keep hearing
persuasions from others.

          Why should I change?

I am a naturalist.

Leave me be.

Because what you are saying is that
I am not accepted as I am,
that I am not accepted for my desire
to be natural.

Natural is what I value.

And I do receive sounds
just enough to dance with grace.

Twenty-three is the deadline.
...and I choose to be natural.

Despair

Sleek black suit with high heels and pearls
Copies of resumes in leather-bound portfolio
Inappropriateness of the phone, keys, and
                desperation safely hidden

Screeching from a disembodied voice
announcing seven rounds of seven minutes,
professional women mentoring potential
protégés, speed mentoring
yet seeking connection in networking

The gleam of pearls dimmed after
countless letters of rejection in wake of failed
interviews, forced appearance of confidence

Insecurity laced with despair seeping through

Wearing the same pearls with fragile hope,
finding that connection, finding mentors
to secure my high heeled footing in the 'Ham
to wash away the years of rejection and
dismissal

Round tables heavily laden with ivory cloth
Chandeliers subtle in their dazzle
Making my way to Table Nine, fragile hope

in my heart, reaching this particular one
Seeking for a way into the dragon's lair

The lair taking up the valley of the 'Ham,
Blazing dragons everywhere, rushing
saving lives, writing grants, connecting
educating minds from all over the world

Praying fervently to be seen worthy
A princess worth saving
Bravely entering the sphere of this one dragon
Tentatively smiling at her neutral stance

Others join Table Nine, their reasons different
yet seeking connection

I should have humbled myself and
sat across the table

Instead of foolishly, arrogantly choosing
the seat next to her. Icebreakers reveal
my foolish imposing

She turns left, to me
indicating that I begin.

I stutter through, scared of how I sound
The neutral face darkens into dismissiveness
Slight angle away from me as she addresses

others, while I turn inward, grasping onto
His hem for dignity

Squawk from the microphone, signaling
next round. Slowly getting up, I slip her card
into my leather-bound portfolio, praying
fervently for the next ones to be better than this

Four rounds in, my mind still pulled to Table
Nine, to that Chief Human Resources Officer.

    Should I?

    Should I?

Biting my lips into a thin line of determination,
I strode purposefully back to Table Nine,
praying fervently,
seeking a way into the dragon's lair,
seeking to be regarded worthy,
a princess worth saving

I softly greet her, "I would like to talk more,
to learn more from you,"

She looks up and sees me.
Wrathful disdain flares from her pores

She does not stop me as I sit down
next to her, again being foolish

Only one other girl joins Table Nine,
Across the table from the leader,
Her sleek blonde shining

Despair sinks lower in my stomach
as the leader angles towards her

Approval emanating from her pores
towards the sleek blonde,
ignoring me

I hug myself within, huddling around
the cracked pieces in my heart,
holding on to His hem for dignity, integrity,
remaining quiet

The sleek blonde grows nervous,
her eyes shifting in my direction
the longer the leader stubbornly refuses
to acknowledge me as she focuses
all her energy on her

Holding on to His hem for dignity, integrity,
remaining quiet

      confused hurt keeps pushing up

Softly, I pose a question.

The leader stiffens.

Without looking at me, she answers
while looking instead at the other,
her voice harder

Holding on to His hem for dignity, integrity,
I withdraw into silence,
waiting to escape the dragon's lair

Not feeling worthy,
Not a princess worth saving

The next round rings out, women switching
tables, speed dating mentors

I rush out, my high heels tightening
running to the Darth Vader,
heart, rapid beating
mind holding tight with bands of despair

Not letting myself think,
My hands gripping the steering wheel
Holding on to His hem for dignity, integrity

Reaching the place of Jaguars
Abruptly parking into place
Sending a text of urgency

Weaving between shining sports utility vehicles
My eyes desperately seeking her long dark hair
Her emerging from the double side doors
She has abruptly ended her class before
the bell even rings

Motioning me to get in her vehicle

Doors shut, and tears of frustration, despair
flood the car, sounds of my sobs anguish

She listens with all her being,
Her eyes taking in the most open,
vulnerable parts of me

Sobbing through words of frustration
of not being regarded worthy
My education not being considered
Interviews hastily end, discouraging
Letters of rejection
The lady from the dragon's lair
Her disdain when I opened my mouth

"Do I need to keep proving my worth?"
"Do I need to keep going to school?"
"Do I need to change myself?"

Her dark eyes watching,
Not saying anything,
Her eyes speaking.

"I should have stayed with him.
He is right. Nobody cares what I have to say.
Nobody understands me," my voice rings,
filling the car.

She shakes her head no – "Forget him."

Jesus said to him,
"Get up, take up your bed, and walk."
– John 5:8 (ESV)

Not only that, but we rejoice in our sufferings, knowing that suffering produces endurance, and endurance produces character, and character produces hope, and hope does not put us to shame, because God's love has been poured into our hearts through the Holy Spirit who has been given to us.
– Proverbs 3:5-6 (ESV)

soul sister's writing

Starlight nights seeping into sunlit mornings,
Sounds of our voices mingling with
                              brain-massaging ideas
Saving the world, the love of hundreds of cats

Super Nintendo days, swimming days
Soul sisters deep to the core
Seeing her, her seeing me

Scribbles in my journals
Strokes of an architect in hers
Soul searching through articulateness

Strokes of her architectural lines
Stirring many, many moments, memories
Sending flushes of thought-provoking
                              conglomeration

Seeing in her articulation, the desire to find a
                              cure
Sensing her yearning for my hearing to
                              crystallize,
Sounds that I could not even imagine,
                              taking in all the sounds

Street, where we grew up next to each other
Striving for greatness, scouting the creek
Stars in the sky when the roof was open

Stories we share in
            scrawling, speaking, showing
Stories she created,
            me having the standard hearing
Standard hearing that the world can only
                        understand

Stories she creates,
            me being transformed over time
Stories she shares,
            her vision dynamic yet with
            determination
Stubborn, she believes, pushing for the best

Strokes of her architectural lines
Splintered wood of upstairs loft,
                        fifth year of college
Securely loved, iron sharpening iron

Scholarship in the marrow of our bones
Steamrolling through on bare bones of sleep
Surging each other on,
            not simply strolling through
Stick it through, stick it,
            a bit of stress a good teacher

Stability in seeing things to completion,
Soar higher with the title,
                    not sink lower without doctorate

Strokes of her architectural lines, words bringing
Strength in the soulness of our bond
Seeing through her eyes, the inspiration

Slides of her established profession,
Sliding into my cognition of her intentions
Spanning over four decades,
                    the soulness of our bond

Strokes of her architectural lines, words bringing
Sameness and hard-earned wisdom together,
                    the cords of three
Staying to the end, tight, not loosely stranded

Sating curiosity,
                    the boy
                    with the white shell necklace,
Scratching the paper with pen,
                    the thirteen ghosts of Alabama
Stories that we weave together,
                    cross country trippin' Savannah

Stories, the intuitiveness we share
Sending soul-felt thoughts, unhindered
Soul sisters that we are

Parallel journeys

Reaching out to my soul sister,
sharing with her my confidences,
my fears, my uncertainties

The rarity of our bond
warms my heart
when I receive her response

Filled with blessings
Filled with her own confidences,
Her fears, her uncertainties

The precision of our soulness
solidify our parallel journeys

Since we do not want the world to know yet
                                this big thing
in our respective lives,
        and we are aligned in that determination
that only two girls growing up next door to each
other could ever comprehend…

we understood each other

no words are needed,
        only love that lasts for infinity

therefore, when her moment arrived,
        I celebrated her

when my moment arrived,
        she celebrated me

Taking the plunge

Father, respecting my wish at twenty-three,
before I master the art of research.

After being the first of the ceremony,
walk across the stage, front-page photo
Mother's turn to insist
that I draw on my research prowess

Stubborn, use that stubbornness and
back up the argument with research, she says

If I still insist on refusing,
at least my foundation is stronger,
having done the research

In my speeches to audiology students,
Timelines,
percentages of my decreased resistance,
and increased knowledge

Reasons, still there, fluctuating:
> *One—natural*
> *Two—vanity, cutting into skull*
> *Three—why better hearing if I have*
> *enough*
> *Four—not wanting to lose the natural*
> *residual hearing*
> *Five—water a stronger hearing aid,*
> *natural*
> *Six—horror stories of others who went*
> *total deaf*
> *Seven—no good descriptions of*
> *transformation experience*
> *Eight—point of no return,* infinity
> *Nine—in denial*
> *Ten—is there such a thing as perfection?*

Eleven months of research, interviews,
meetings,
> sharing thoughts with my sunrise,
> the one who instills within me a vision
of what could
> be

Praying over these uncertain, fear-filled reasons
with my Sonrise of the One who is with me,
leading up to October seventeenth

October seventeenth,
                my firstborn nephew

Central-timezoned October seventeenth,
Eastern-timezoned October eighteenth,
                my lastborn nephew
The hour of midnight,
          many stubborn arguments from me

The twelfth month filled with rehearsing
Writing, rewriting, reciting,
letting the words flow
from my mouth, praying to be understood…

Praying to be accepted,
Praying to be chosen,
Praying to have hope again,
Praying to have a voice,
Praying to be heard,
Praying to be listened,
Praying to have a voice,

To speak with conviction
To speak with hope
To speak with knowledge
To speak with courage that others would want
to hear
what I have to say, abolishing the cacophonous,
accusing voices from the past chapter

To show the world
that I have a voice

That my voice matters

That expressing my voice matters

Knees shaking hard as I plunged through
the four minutes seeming so long
yet perfect as previous speaker and coach
Anne encouraged me

the four minutes of giving my all,
disciplining my voice to have strength
as my brain commands the pacing
of my spoken words

the four minutes of giving my all
knees shaking hard
keeping my high heels stubbornly planted
in the thin carpet,
seeing four rows of listening faces

the four minutes of giving my all
ended with a relieved smile,
struggling to tamper down the shakes
crawling to the metal folding chair

Accepting the hand of my fellow auditioner
An encouraging handshake
Affirming words as we slip out of the room,
into the night to wait for the email

October seventeenth, the night of that email

Curving my mind into engaging conversation
with the sunrise of my friend, absorbing his
experiences, education, encouragement
when a notification of that email slides
across the screen

Remembering the shakes in my knees
Feeling the tremor in my insides
The four minutes of giving my all

Being seen, my voice being heard
Conviction in my expression accepted
Chosen to join the cohort
Chosen to stand on the red dot

A smile takes over not only my face,
also my entire being, in my heart

October seventeenth, my decision
to take the plunge has been made

Sharing with the sunrise of my friend,
                    –the one who calls me "Doc"
        "I am taking the plunge."

He quickly responds,
        "What made you decide to do it?"

        "I will be a TEDx speaker."

Our conversation ensues
well into the morning,

The sunrise of encouragement, altruism
True as always, his words make me smile more,

The Sonrise of hope instilled within me,
more tangible to my awareness than ever.

The surgery

Text my parents the news:
>   *TEDx talk, taking the plunge*

Not going into conversation
Or, I would back out

Surgery when? Halloween
That's your niece's birthday
>   …and the lastborn nephew has been
>   born this morning,
>   at a controversial time zoned hour of
>   midnight
Please wait to have the surgery

Back and forth
Yield
Move surgery to Monday before Thanksgiving

Meet with speaker coach
Flesh out the script
Tighten the focus

Sharing with students before the break
that I would return different, healing

Parents with the truck and trailer,
Guy friends with their muscles

Moving out of the posh skybox of a place
Moving to a smaller Bavarian place
at the feet of Vulcan,
the statue overlooking the city,
soon to be my watchguard

Boxes full of dishes, utensils
Clothes already in their own room
at the Bavarian place

Spending the last night
Thinking about the surgery
Dropping the keys off at five in the morning

Climbing in the Darth Vader,
My walk of death for a part of me,
Reaching the point of no return
                        No more conversation
                        Or, I would back out

Rustling hospital gown
Billowy metallic blankets from the outer space
Inclined bed, loopiness setting in
Interacting with the surgery team
Reading scrawled *"I love you Aunt Sarahs"*
on folded cardboard paper
Many family members in the waiting room,
I felt their presence through the walls

Videoing myself to WhatsApp a video text
to the one traveling across the world
  Her graceful cat, now in my care,
  living at the new Bavarian place
Her immediate videoed response,
  supporting my bravery
Her smile shining bright, eyes sparkling
She knew the doctor, trusts me in his good care

Handing my phone over to the last one
  I allow to be in the room with me
Lifelong friend with long dark hair
in her favorite purple
  Sitting, witness to the before and after
  Scolding me for flirting with the doctor
  Am I flirting? I am not aware
My droopiness pulling me under

Awareness, a planetarium of awakening
White light, a tap on my sternum
My eyes flutter open

It's done.

I took the plunge.

I changed.

In the bubbles, disoriented

Cupping the shaved right side of my head,
Expansively covering the ear,
Stark whiteness, roughly punctuated
Blood seeping through the bandaged cloth

Parents hovering over me,
      Watchful over my intake of pain pills
      No need, I stop after the first two days

An icepick-piercing pain,
Long icepick needle sitting firm, sending
synaptic sparks of protest

Vulnerability rages as I stare at the photo
on my phone after my mother took it

Ebony dark hard stitches
Embedded in the shaved skin,
Curved above, around the ear

Recalling the words of my blonde warrioress
To do one side, the right side, the dominant side
Only one side

She knew me well
          She knew my penchant
          for au naturale hearing-wise
The left being my natural one, amplified sweet

Recalling the admiration in the eyes
of the doctor as he explained the rarity
of me as the perfect candidate:
Born profound bilateral sensorineural deaf
Wore hearing aids consistently
Used my aided residual hearing well

Tender touches on the black stitches
Feeling their prick
          as Aurora did with the needle of a
          spinning wheel
Like Aurora, things have changed
The point of no return

Same as with wisdom teeth pulled in Biloxi
Same as with my feline daughter dying
          in my sister's arms
The point of no return
Blood seeping through the stark whiteness

Taking the plunge
Hitting the surface of the water hard
Resulting chaos of waves, pushing beyond
the familiarity, the comfort

Feeling the underwater waterfall of bubbles
Hugging my plunging form
into the depths of unknown

Only one side, the left side—hearing aid
My guiding sound
for the next four weeks

Must swim back up,
through the crowding bubbles
to seek familiarity

In the everyday routine,
Washing the dried blood away
Drying my hair into its caramel honey tresses,
Covering the shaved part, not letting the world
see nor know

Seeking familiarity

Among the turkey and dressing, cornbread,
cranberry sauce, pumpkin pie, sweet tea

Among the prayers and thanksgivings,
reading books, playing board games

Among the tailgate crowds
of navy and burnt orange
Roars of *War Eagles*

Holding on to the familiarity
Protecting myself from questions
Protecting myself from the reality
By not sharing this part of me
with the world
            —only those close to me know for now

But: flat levels / no volume

Monday before Christmas, the day of activation
More people filled up the waiting room
Family and friends as witnesses

Two audiologists calling me in
I sit, a notebook open on my lap
Attitude simmering underneath,
Dealing with the reality of the point of no return
No longer au naturale in the right
Holding onto the naturalness in the left

Not knowing what to expect
The audiologists warn me over and over again
to not have expectations

No one experience can be shared by another
My own experience
while warned against having expectations

Struggling to forget the stories that I have
listened to or read of others' experiences,
although I stopped doing
research since I made the decision to take the
plunge.

The curse of a strong memory, recounting
others' experiences—particularly that of a man
with two homes,
            one in Utah and another in Maine.
            He lost all of his hearing;
            his CI worked for a few years, then
            dropped to nothingness.

Struggling against expectations
…and failing

The audiologists look at the computer,
talking in low tones
that my left-sided hearing aid picks up,
then looking at me, neutral expressions

Crackling sensation spreads through the nerves,
from the heart, the core, startling me,
being strummed like a guitar,
confounding me with the lack of sound.

Energy, one audiologist explains

But

Energy?

Volume, I demand

But

Is this actually activation? I speak—*zap*

This shock collar clamps around my neck

I struggle to speak—*more zaps*

What is this? I stare at them—*another zap*

At their neutral professional nods, I feel trapped
in this crackling, guitar-strumming sensation,
the shock collar

I control my breathing, looking down at the
notebook and starting to write, reflecting,
gathering my
scattered thoughts, not wanting to vocalize

But

I feel punished

Taking the plunge to live out the message
I am crafting to share on the red dot,
for the audience to understand me better,
to speak more clearly,
to take responsibility
for improving the way I communicate

taking the plunge = irony

the morning stretches into four hours
as family and friends take turns
to be in the room, their presence
both bewildering and encouraging

But

I feel trapped, frustrated
Struggling to articulate

Crackling sensations, guitar strumming
Sounds of a gong, slamming synapses
Whenever I speak, shock collar

No sounds bouncing from the eardrum,
as a hearing aid would do, amplify
residual hearing

Rather, the connection from the synaptic
patterns to the core of my being

Without the volume, without the energy
I feel hollow, not being able to grasp
tangibility of sound that I had expected
from the eardrum

I form my words, to describe this
weirdness, the need to have sound,

What I am experiencing is not sound
I am stunned with this reality if this is how
standard people are hearing, then they are weird,

What is the point of having eardrums?

The analogy – analog to digital to cloud…

> *Instead of the* tangibility
> of saving files on the desktop,
intangibility of the cloud snatching up the files,
having to find those files in the cloud

The core, the nervous system being the cloud
The eardrum, the desktop

Please turn on the volume, I beg

The audiologists shake their heads:
> You need to train your brain to listen
> what you are experiencing
> Then we will turn it on in a few months

Writing more on my spiral notebook,
gathering thoughts, making sense of this
unexpected, unfamiliar territory of hearing

The other audiologist watches,
          sensing my state of mind,
          gently asks if we could do a hearing test

At my resigned nod,
          she covers her mouth
          and says,

          "baseball"

          "car"

          "popcorn"

To my dismay, I understand her clearly.

But

In denial, I beg for the volume, the energy,
to be turned on

She shakes her head no, then seeing the
stubbornness in my jaw, asks me to take off the
processor,
          put the hearing aid in the left

Quickly pulling the processor off the right side,
Hearing aid in the left ear

She covers her mouth and speaks.
An audiological technique, so familiar,
yet so undecipherable

I do not understand her, attempting
to look confident by guessing which word

Seeing my eyes, she nods at the processor

Shoulders slumped, while sliding the processor
on my right side, feeling it clamp onto the
magnet

Looking back into her eyes, I wait.
She covers her mouth and speaks.

      "baseball"

More emotions pushing against
the back of my eyeballs

I lower my head
into my hands and sob

I pull myself together before looking back in her
eyes
        Promise of consistency with
        auditory-verbal therapy
        Then, turn on the volume sooner

Nodding my agreement, I finally decide to leave
the office and face the world.

She smiles and stands up to hug me,
        whispering with tears in her eyes,
The people in the waiting room have been here
all morning for you. I have not seen any other
person having this much support.

                You
                can
                do
                this

                No more *buts.*

Synaptic sparkles

Lunch after activation
Friends and family wanting to
continue gathering, to be
there for me as I adjust

my new normal

Babalu's – its signature sparkling wand
mirroring the synaptic sparkles
within, euphoric crackling

Euphoria, guitar-strumming erotic
No wonder why I did not wake up
until today

No wonder why I did not get it
when people stop and shout,
"That's my favorite song!"
then lip-sync, sing along

The sounding gong, the core
that clangs upon the soul—music

I ask my support system:
"Do you listen with your ears or
with your body?"

Guacamole made tableside
avocado, sun-dried tomato,
red & green onions, kosher salt,
cilantro, lime juice, fresh jalapeños,
bacon—guacamole made tableside

Southern cuisine with Latin flair
Creole tacos and tapas, beef burgers
Well-deserved cucumber jalapeño margarita

Enunciating, "I want a margarita"

Bringing over the sparkling wand lit up
from a glass tequila bottle
A celebration of my courage
Of my taking the plunge
To live out my message
on the red dot

Not able to do a total 180

New Bavarian place at the foot of the Vulcan
cars roaring by

My parents not liking the location
wishing that I stayed at the posh skybox
overlooking the Railroad Park and Regions Field

Shrugging off their concerns
always wanted to live for a short while
at this cozy Bavarian-style Manor Village

To see the valley of the city
To see the city skyline
To see the glittering lights at night
at the foot of the 56-foot statue
upon a 124-foot pedestal,
totaling 180 feet

Not able to do a total 180 on the past chapter
Not able to do a total 180 with my quarters
Not able to do a total 180 from the surgery
Not able to do a total 180 from the activation

After hanging the 32-inch decoration of a TV
        The only gift from the past, unasked for
        Yet a gift that could be used for
        relearning, for auditory-verbal therapy
My parents leaving

Jane arriving, walking me through sounds
of my new living quarters
to acclimate to the sounds of traffic,
my irritation, their concerns

I will be fine
I will just have to deal with this new normal
Not able to do a total 180 from all this

A motorcycle roars by,
bringing me to euphoria
My new favorite sound,
most favorite sound in the world,
in my new normal

Unexpected gift

Grumpiness with the new reality
Burrowing my chilled toes
      into the loveseat cushions
Red felt stockings,
      names in green on white tops,
      hanging from the dark pine wood mantle

The Christmas tree in the other room,
      where the nieces and nephews watch
      holiday movies

tucked away in a quiet room,
      the lastborn newborn nephew sleeping

Two siblings in conversation
my interrupting them,
saying something with attitude,
ignoring zaps from the shock collar, albeit
softer the more I am used to them

      At some point while I am speaking,
my sister looks at our brother,
exchanging a particular look.

"What? What's that look for?"
                              I grumpily ask.

After exchanging another look,
she gestures to her lips, explaining,
              "Your speech is clearer."

Curso intensive para **Córdoba, Argentina**

Julie, help me learn Spanish
En cinco días vuelo a Córdoba

Her driving two hours to Auburn
A crash course over margaritas
and tacos at Laredo's

First thing to know: **raw egg drop vowels**

A – E – I – O – U

Vertical sounding of vowels
Holding a raw egg when saying "o"

Do not say "ooh" when saying "u"
Must be "uh" – raw egg drop the vowel

puro = pure
púrpura = purple
purgatorio = purgatory

Open vowels, vertical—not horizontal

Roman = Italian, Spanish, French
Latin = Greek
Aramaic = Greek, Hebrew
Western Europe…
          Romance/Ludo European Language

Yo soy norteamericana

Manana voy at aeropuerto

Yo necesito un taxi a las ocho de la noche

Tienes untaxi gratis to del hotel, complimentario

¿Cómo estás?

Bien, gracias

Later learned the soundness of Julie's teaching,
that I need to understand the cultural background
to learn the language [Spain, Mexico, South
America]

Crisp consonants

Seven days after the day of activation
The day after my siblings declared
that my speech improved

The feel of the wheels under the suitcase
Rolling across the shiny floors of any airport
The sounds the same in any airport

ATL waiting for the flight
At the piano, having my Ferrari moment

Flying from ATL to MEX
Ten-hour layover,
waiting for connecting flight to EZE,
bonded with Jazmine,
a college sophomore in Connecticut,
seeing her on the phone, speaking in Spanish
reaching for her, asking for help,
since the airport people are kicking us out
from the gate areas

We huddle together on a concrete bench,
next to the grass area
beyond the security point
in the coldest airport in the world

The designed holes in the concrete walls,
through which the harsh winds pummel our skin,
her wanting to watch my talk,
which would happen in three months,
her willing to listen to me rehearse,
my listening to her feedback,
my sharing with her
about my taking the plunge
my Ferrari

From MEX to EZE
A six-hour layover, a quick text urging me
to taxi over to see the city skyline of Bueno
Aires from the rooftops

The sounds the same in any airport
Yet the currency not the same
        No dollars…*pesos*
        No credit cards…*pesos*
        I do not have any *pesos*
        Must be *pesos*

Could not read their lips in Spanish
Instead, reading their body language
Taking cues from their emotions
Smiling at them, smiling from my heart,
Appealing to their hearts

$50 flat rate, yellow Fiat radio taxi
Conductor and I struggling to communicate
how to get to Aspen Square Palmero Soho
Conductor hugging me, kissing me on the cheek

Hugging Krystal, meeting Kiwi and Dina
The glittering city lights, the never-ending
neon-glowing traffic
in the wee hours of the morning

Taxi back to the airport
The sun rising, lifting me up
from EZE to COR

No ear-popping at all throughout
Weird that only that my left ear ached from
an impending cold, nothing in my right ear

Delighted discovery that the right ear
is not stuffed up like the left ear from the cold.
Sounds crystal clear even with a cold

Upon arriving, Gaby's AirBnb
Two days all to myself
Waiting for the dark-eyed, curly haired Krystal,
the mother of Miss Grace, to follow
from Bueno Aires with her Earharts

Two days all to myself
WhatsApping Gaby about her bathroom,
Since I could not read Spanish
Her neighbor messages me,
Letting Pablo in to check the bathroom

After thirty long befuddled minutes
His eyes watchful, his fingers tapping on the
phone Google Translate, our best friend

Laughing, I engage
He explains the intricacies of the bathroom

Once solved, I explore the sidewalks
of Córdoba,
Finding myself in the Biblioteca district,
        ending up at Joan's recommended
        Córdoba Public Library
black and white marble, intricacy in the wood,
books filling my senses

Two days all to myself
Interacting in miscommunication with the locals
Dancing with the Remote Year Veritas
on their last night in Córdoba

Two days pass, and the door opens
There she is, the dark-eyed beauty with her
strength and determination to be free,
followed by Remote Year Earharts

Landscape full of tangoing couples, old
architecture, steeples of churches, and parks,
trees shading us
from the eye-searing sunlight

The next several days swirl by in a carnivorous
haze washed down with sparkling water,
Malbec,
and occasional fernets

Exploring everywhere, the cracked sidewalks
One time, kiss one of them, pop back right up,
striding on in stilettos, no fuss,
to a restaurant, where white tablecloths reign

New Year's Eve filled to the brim
with digital nomads, meaningful conversations,
Italian cooking, champagne toasts
around the coworking space,
Tears and shouts of *Happy New Years*
and *Feliz Año Nuevos*

New day, new year, new beginning
One-on-one conversations with wisdom
Rehearsing my talk,
which would take place on Krystal's birthday
they promising to watch my talk
as part of celebrating Krystal

Funneling down to the two of us,
Sitting at the long table,
the windows wide open,
the sun sitting with us,
Others still sleeping in,
Realness in our conversation,
My sharing the weirdness
of my new normal

   "Your consonants are crisp," she states
   as she pulls out another Sour Patch Kid
   piece from the crinkly yellow bag

Sparkling mineral water with filet mignon
Pushes pesos into my hand
  before hugging my neck
  sending me off to the aeropuerto,
  reversing the itinerary

This time a twenty-three-hour layover
in Ciudad de México, where I follow
        Aaron's K.I.S.S. method
        of doing one special thing:
        an appetizer and a drink by the pool
        under a yellow umbrella

Staying at the historical
Gran Hotel Ciudad de México,
its elegance framed by the Zócalo,
its presence famed by James Bond,
the festive atmosphere from
the lingering holidays

New day, new year, new beginning
New normal with encouraging friends who say
that my consonants are crisp

Ferrari

Hard adjustment
Brain not understanding, not receptive
to the sound waves

Left-sided hearing aid, au naturale
help with the transformation, transition
modulate my voice
alleviate the impact of sound waves,
ease that acute sensation, the shock collar

Electrifying myself

shifting gears
no longer automatic
now manual

Jane shifts my perspective
mid-life crisis, perhaps
not a Corvette
rather, a Ferrari

hers is the Corvette
—Ferrari, mine to handle

Shifting gears
with each mapping

First mapping one month later:
Tell the Audis to give me volume

After shifting more, ask for more volume
Shifting up several more levels
Until they say, wait until the next mapping
in two months and two weeks

Two weeks after I give the talk

The night before, 70-80% accuracy
After first mapping, 90-100% accuracy

Pick up the hissing *Sss* better
Still needing work on numbers though

Jane suggesting to Josie
that I need to take the Ferrari out for a spin
Sister gifts me a CD package of classic music
to distinguish between instruments

For the Ferrari, for the road

Sunrise at three

Sitting on a box filled with favorite novels
Texting with a smile on my face
Laughing with warmth in my heart
Reading his words across the screen

White walls with a glossy sheen, glow
In the sparkles of the night, glow
As the sun rises, glow
As my smiles continue

Books shipped overseas, uplifting
Those in need, while fraught with
Years long civil unrest, uplifting
with the determination to ensure their
literacy needs

Sparking my admiration for him,
          the one who calls me "Doc"
Sun rising, my heart rising with respect
Shimmering in hopefulness
Sincerely

His voice shaping the spirit, the soul within
Forming the strength of his tendons,
As I gaze out of the window, seeing Vulcan
standing guard as Aurora glows into white

His words, his voice beckoning
Turning my gaze down to see more
Of his words, soaked with truthfulness
Of honeyed listening, sharing
Hopefulness with sincerity
Leaning into the curves of his typed words
Having found that core of connection

Rising from the box filled with favorite novels
Smiling, knowing that I am seen
As I am, and now I am rising from within
The courage to…

Stretch to dimension three
Of possibility

Relearning and rehearsing

Rehearsing the talk
Relearning through auditory-verbal therapy
Listening and speech therapy

Long dark-haired Jane pushing
for one hundred percent perfection, accuracy
capturing the long and short {Ling} sounds:
    ah, ehh, ooh, mm, ss, sh
her vast experience as a stepmom, aunt, and
friend of others who took the plunge

Even though I was the first one
    with hearing impairment
    that she and her sister have ever met
Ginger, my transliterator, mother of one
Jane, my lifelong friend, fierce supporter

Jane not giving up on me
when I yearn to…
    rest from the relearning,
    rest from cognitively listening,
    rest from tensing up my stomach
    when enunciating the letters *j* and *ch*

rehearse the talk instead

Rehearse, rehearse, rehearse
Speaker coach Anne—patient, pacing me,
reminding me to enunciate certain words

Going back to auditory-verbal therapy,
working on listening
for the multi-syllable words
and hard letters of *S, J, V, F, Z*
numbers, word pairs of ling sounds
hoot and *hot,*
peak and *meek,*
shake and *snake,*
tiger and *panther,*
movie and *groovy,*
names of my siblings, mixing *Brad* and *Sarah*
names of my diamonds, mixing *Jane* and *Sarah*
her Southern drawl

in my talk, worked on enunciating
connection
communication
frustration
patience
Girl Scouts
reach
push
Pepsi
responsibility
disconnected

after all, yes *after all*
Sexy Stacey scoops seashells from the sea
Jefferson State Community College
consulting
S – Sampson, sissy, yes
J – Josie, Jane, college
V – veal, vehemence
F – after, fun, fool
Z – zebra, realize, verbalize

Enunciating, rehearsing the talk
Speaker coach Anne helping not only with
the pacing, memorization
also the enunciation

Her coaching part of positioning
the cameras at right moments

Must have every single word
enunciated and memorized
for the audience

> I took the plunge **not** for myself,
> *I took the plunge **for** the audience*
> *I relearned **for** the audience*
> *I rehearsed **for** the audience*

the two audiologists pleased
with the spreadsheet that
Jane and I created,
finally turning on the volume,
switching me on, making my world
savoring the hissing sounds of *Sss* and *Zzz*

New Normal

When Brad, Beth, and I were together,
playing outside
they were chatting

I tuned them out,
busy crafting a wreath
out of yellow dandelions

The excitement in their voices
pulled me back into the conversation

> "Imagine if you wake up, not deaf…all
> the noises you get to hear would
> overwhelm you."

____

Fast forward to three decades later,
Here I am, overwhelmed by the symphony
Of crickets, frogs, mockingbirds, owls

Initial sound experiences:

The unwelcome white noise of
Buzzes, hums, drones, vrooms
from appliances, air conditioning

I cannot stand the white noise
I slip off my hearing devices
for a moment of peace and quiet,
Not good for my relearning,
for my auditory-verbal therapy

Picking up sounds without striving:
Sss
Beeps of credit card machines,
            remote unlocking, microwave
Ticking of the blinkers and light
            switches—which I thoroughly detest
Scritching of pumice stone rubbing the sole of
            my friend's foot
Air flowing from vents
Ice clacking inside glass
Paper rustling
Potato chip bags crinkling

Others' observation:

Crispiness of my consonants
Enunciation
More melody in my voice
More feminine
Less harsh

Need to relax when relearning

My observation:

Never thought spoken language would emanate
so strongly through sound waves. No wonder I
did not understand science with its energy,
Physics, and that I preferred Chemistry. Sound
waves must be actively listened for…otherwise,
the brain would not receive the synapses, to pick
up sound waves.

Bubble bath congruence: when enjoying a hot
bubble bath for a long time, the heat and bubbles
fade away, requiring our active efforts to revive
them back into being.

Other congruences:

Tornado: pull out certain sounds (car, house)

Left-handed brother: his arm cut off, forcing
him to learn how to write with his right hand, yet
his handwriting will not be the same

Visual impaired: rearranging the furniture in the
room, forcing the individual with visual
impairment adjust to the different flow of the
room

Change the question:

Can you hear me?
Irritation rises

Can you hear me?
Reining in patience

Yes, I always have
Otherwise, I would not have this leverage
Look at how I dance, how the gracefulness of
my body curves in accordance with the rhythm

Reword that question:
How are you hearing?

Slushy *Sss* no more

threeS into infinity

The hiss, lingering

Red Dot

read out loud,
rehearse the scripted talk
receive feedback, work on transitions
relearn speech patterns

provide Pepsi moments through writing prompts
prove the validity of my message
persist in overcoming frustration
to improve communication

after having closed the past chapter
after having lived in the 'Ham
after having traveled the Freedom Tour
something deep inside that needs to speak
share with others about pushing past boundaries,
past fears,
past inadequacies,
with hope in our hearts

the strong possibility of being on the stage,
on the red dot

practice, rehearse
transform, relearn

discover the quality in relationships
as I hold Gran's dying hand
while reading out loud
the draft of my talk, knowing that she would
clap her hands, smile in exclamation, saying,
        "Well, I declare
        oh how beautiful you are!"

Pull through the practices,
Practice, memorize numerous times a day
Something about the humming noises
        of the road
Something about the rain hitting the windshield
        when I drive, surging me on

Make Gran proud,
Make speaker coach Anne proud,
Make Jane proud,
Make my blonde warrioress proud,
Make Dr. Pappas proud,
Make my Audis proud,
Make my parents, family, friends proud,
Make Matthew, Rebecca, Suzan, Gabriel proud
Make Krystal proud, feel celebrated and
        connected across the equator on her
birthday
        when I deliver the talk on the red dot

in the two weeks leading up to the red dot,
been struggling to rehearse,
Anne notices and switches gears,
        telling me to enjoy the process,
        have fun, stop practicing

Smiling at Rebecca
        as we high-fived each other in passing,
Stepping onto the red dot
The lavalier mic clasped to my collar
Feeling centered on the red dot

A sound crashes,
I look out in the audience,
waiting to see if I should wait

No one moves,
I move into speaking,
still waiting for another sound to drop

Hearing my voice amplified,
Yet mechanical, guttural

Nothing I can do about these
        startling distractions
The dress rehearsal did not prepare me for this

Focusing on pacing myself, speaking
the well-rehearsed, well-memorized words

concentrating more on enunciation
rather than the content
immersing into body language, warming up
knowing that at least seven cameras are poised
to portray my facial expressions and motions
from different angles for the audience to see
my face up close as part of my message

feeling warmth as peace radiates through my
limbs while I speak

I am the message of my talk
I am the visual of my talk
I am living out the talk

I took the plunge for the audience

What I learned from having taken the plunge:
enjoy the process

Ambassador,
TEDxBirmingham 2017: Possibility

Speaker,
TEDxBirmingham 2018: BeforeXAfter

The Crayon Analogy

Standing before Audi students,
Sharing the transformative experiences

Waking up the body, waking up the synapses
Relearning through auditory-verbal therapy

Cognitive dissonance:
The uncomfortable feelings we experience
whenever we hold two or more contradictory
beliefs about ourselves, or when we act in ways
that are incongruent with our inner beliefs and
values. When we have contradicting beliefs and
behaviors, it creates an uncomfortable stress that
forces us to seek internal consistency, either by
changing the incongruous behavior or
abandoning the inconsistent belief.

Work through cognitive dissonance,
relearn through auditory-verbal therapy
Consistent until my brain is forced
to abandon those self-sabotaging beliefs
that no longer serve me

Congruent to a hot bubble bath
If sitting still, the water cools
Need to cause ripples to feel the remaining heat

Same with sound waves
Must actively listen to messages sent to my
brain for the pathways to strengthen into
recognized hearing

Like pictures of silhouettes emanating heat
waves, feel sound waves emanating from my
body

Inside radio, static envision sound waves coming
to life visually
            Reverberation

Sound waves travel
Traveling is education
Travel the sound waves

Courage to keep traveling, to let go of trying to
do a total 180,
No matter the dangers
Ask for help, do not be afraid to ask for help
Not be afraid to level up

Classical music, taking the Ferrari out for a spin

Taking the plunge physically and neurologically,
I declare as my gaze takes in the room full of
Audis

Courage to view humility as a virtue, not pride
Humility to bring down my arrogance about
previously held ideas and worldview about
hearing

Timing
Frequency
Modulation
Inflection
Energy = volume = intensity of sound

Why stay with three primary colors of red, blue,
and yellow?

The hearing aid can only be the sharpest with the
freshest, newest batteries
The primary colors = *three* frequencie*ss, threeS*
Move beyond *threeS* primary colors
Perspective too trichromatic,
          even monochromatic

The yearning to hear more,
          green, purple, and orange

There are more crayons of possibilities
There are more crayons of communicating

Metallic, pastel, glitter,
          inspired by food, nature, and more

A whole spectrum of colors

Colors = frequencies

The cochlear implant,
          sharper than the hearing aid
          more frequencies,
          multichromatic, highly pigmented

I can only imagine there being many colors that
I have never seen before,
          Auditory-verbal therapeutic needs

The trichromatic-painted canvas needs more
coloring.

Auditory-verbal therapy will splash more
coloring onto the canvas, build upon it

threeS into infinity
of colors,
of frequencies,
of possibilities

__Presentation:__ *"Why I decided to take the plunge: The decision-making journey of going with cochlear implant"*

Wednesday, 16 January 2019
Auburn University, AuD Students and Professors

CI = cochlear implant

__Responses from the Audis:__

♦ *"I find it very interesting to hear the point of view of someone who was against CIs but not part of the Deaf community"*

♦ *"I was saddened when you told the part about the HR lady being standoffish"*

♦ *"It's important that we know what people go through during the process of receiving and adjusting to CIs"*

♦ *"Very enlightening to hear about the steps you took to make your decision and the specific fears you had"*

♦ *"She provided new insights. I never had anyone explain from their perspective why/how they made this decision. It was very personal and explained so well"*

♦ *"She walked me through all aspects and painted a very clear image of what she experienced and how she made her decision"*

♦ *"She provided insight but with humor and a realistic portrayal of herself. It made the presentation not only informative but memorable"*

♦ *"It was a deep topic, you made us really think of how much this process can affect a person"*

♦ *"Why did your family decide not to use ASL or opt for a CI when you were growing up? Why did they choose Cued Speech instead?"*

♦ *"Dr. Moreman truly brought us into her story and made us feel like we were there. I could feel the emotions"*

♦ *"Sometimes, doctors or clinicians don't pay enough importance to their patients' needs and concerns. It is a big and important decision to make for any patient and we as caregivers*

*should provide the correct information and
respect the people's will"*

♦ *"Each CI recipient has a different experience.
I appreciate your honesty, as an adult,
describing the challenges you faced with society
and how it played a role in your decision"*

♦ *"I was so proud our students had the
opportunity to hear Dr. Moreman today. It is
invaluable to hear the experience firsthand. I
feel this talk will have a profound impact on how
our students practice Audiology in the future.
She has an amazing ability to articulate emotion
in an educational manner. Dr. Moreman
captured everyone's attention and provided vivid
insight into her thoughts and feelings throughout
her journey"*

♦ *"The only experience I have had is with
younger children receiving CIs and it's not
exactly a choice THEY make. This was very
eye-opening, and I appreciate Dr. Moreman
sharing her story."*

Experiential

Stepping away from the red dots connecting
the *journey-esque* decision of taking the plunge,

the previous twenty-one
a tight foundational poetic narrative
of why I took the plunge

More moments spanning over time
before and after, *as the theme of*
TEDxBirmingham 2018: BeforeXAfter

the **before** pieces of writing signify the time and
thoughts before taking the plunge

the **after** pieces of writing signify the time and
thoughts after having taken the plunge

messy, yet necessary
to share sound perception

messy, yet necessary
slushiness of saying *Sss*, the piercing sharpness
of *Shhh*

gaining insight from one
whose moments of before and after

the sound perception
what is true hearing?

we know what we experience
whatever God chooses to give

what is true hearing?
as God creates it or what the regulars claim

the sound perception
shared in the narrative

the narrative being experiential
in *before* and *after* moments, not organized

more stream of consciousness
parallel to perceiving sounds

Cascade effect

Although this is my journey
        experiential, explorative

NOT ALONE, *definitely not alone*

        my narrative,
        filled with family, friends, fellows
                joys in celebration
                        tears in memorials

        my sound perception silhouetted by
        others' observations,
                moments shared with others,
                        words honoring others'
                                roles in my journey

a tapestry of individual and collaborative efforts
        seeking significance in understanding

about sound
        about hearing
                about listening
                        about faith without
                                sound

                        about faith without
                                hearing

                        about faith without
                                listening

these works are not simply about me,
        they are about the cascade effect,
                    about becoming better

in other words,
my auditory-verbal therapy,
cochlear implant adjustment journey
        could not and would not have been
        successful without others
not without the foundation
        of my parents' decisions
not without the foundation
        of my sound perception,
                    both *before and after*

What is it about pearls?
after

•

More refined and precious
than rubies, emeralds,
and even diamonds
can ever be,
       pearls, the only gemstone
       created within a living creature.

•

No cutting or polishing is needed,
       because pearls are naturally complete
       and lustrous.

•

Created by God through nature,
       pearls symbolize wisdom
       gained through experience.

•

Pearls also represent
       calmness,
       integrity,
       loyalty,
       and purity.

•

Pearls should be protected as valuable treasures.

•

Pearls should not be given without careful
thought and prayer.

•

Margarites (pearls in Greek) are wisdom, words
of great value.

•

*I remember a story about a father
asking his little girl to give him her fake
pearls. She refused each time he asked
until one day she finally said yes. He
thanked her, taking her fake pearls. He
then surprised her by placing a necklace
of real pearls around her neck. The little
girl understood.*

Like that little girl, I understand.

Wednesday, 8 November 2022

Pearls through taking the plunge and relationships

Blessings of wisdom | Proverbs 8

eine Steinbrücke in Deutschland
| a stone bridge in Germany
before

"Put these in the guitar case," my father says
A few coins gleam in his hand,
      waiting to drop and land on my hand

   "Why?"

   "Go and do it. You'll see."

Coins dropping onto my upraised palm

My eyes seeing a lone guy in dark clothing
      ein Gitarrenkoffer liegt geöffnet zu
          seinen Füßen
     a guitar case laying open at his feet
The lone guy not speaking or doing anything

Looking back at my father
Uncertainty holding me back
Curiosity pulling me forward, walking
      über die Kurve der Steinbrücke
      Over the curve of the stone bridge
Large cobblestones,
their gray against the whiteness
of sunlit, overcast sky

Not looking at the stranger, not saying a word
Instead, watching the coins slip from my hand
        In den Gitarrenkoffer, der offen zu
            seinen Füßen liegt
        into the guitar case laying open
            at his feet

Turning back, walking back
        über die Kurve der Steinbrücke
        Over the curve of the stone bridge
Standing next to my father, mother, sister,
Uncle Bill, Aunt SuSu, and cousins Warner and
baby AnnaSmith

His voice, the melody piercing the air,
        Reaching past the limitations
            of my hearing aids
        to the marrow of my hearing perception
        the chambers of my heart,
            the true hearing

        eine eindringliche Melodie
            von der Steinbrücke
        haunting melody from the stone bridge

        Der Sommer meines
            süßen sechzehnten Geburtstags
        the summer of my sweet sixteen

the chambers of my heart, three decades later,
holding
        eine eindringliche Melodie
            von der Steinbrücke
        haunting melody from the stone bridge

even surgically enhanced with more frequencies,
the chambers of my heart, the true hearing
holding
        eine eindringliche Melodie
           von der Steinbrücke
        haunting melody from the stone bridge

His voice, the chambers of my heart, the true
hearing
        falls ich eines Tages
           wieder erleben sollte
        if ever someday to experience again,

        den Verlauf des Verständnisses
           von wahrem Hören und
           Wahrnehmung empfangen
        receive course of understanding true
        hearing and perception

Summer 1996 – the summer I was sixteen
My parents, sister Josie, and I spent three weeks in
England and Germany

Germany: Uncle Bill, Aunt SuSu, and cousins Warner
and AnnaSmith lived there due to Uncle Bill's USAF
career

Mijn Nederlandse Neer
| *My Dutch Gentleman*
before

Emailing every week, letters of endearment
      Long with wonder, across the ocean

      Mijn Nederlandse Neer
      My Dutch Gentleman

Three weeks, global serving
      Amsterdam 2000, Billy Graham

Trains back and forth
      from Utrecht to Amsterdam and back

Streaming under the building-high
      black-and-white theatre photography of
Chicago actors

Warehouses full of metal bunkbeds,
      crates of bottled water

Cold showers, same breakfasts
      of ham, poundcake, and cheese

Farmer's Market, tasting Dutch cheese, Edam
      Mamma Mia gesture,
      huge block of Gouda

Media center, transcribing alongside my mother,
      I yell for her attention by saying,
                "Jo-ann"

Google, a Spaniard enunciated, introducing
          me to the innovative search engine

Crew of Dutch, herding us Americans
          on trains in the morning, in the evening

Changing trains, exchanging smiles
          willingness to try

One coming forward, asking for me
          riding with him and his sister
          to his parents

His father's boat out in the North Sea
          home cooked lunch and dinner
          with his parents and sister

Showing me all of Holland miniature-style,
          'cause I asked to see everything,
          for tulips, the windmills

Walking on the beach,
          seeing the WWII fortifications,
          the tall grasses on the dunes

Listening to his perception of communication,
          his fluency in several languages

Entrancement with his completely
          understanding me,
          no barrier, no misunderstanding

Listening with ease,
     guiding me to be confident in speaking,
     his eyes, understanding the nuances
                   in my speech

The feeling of acceptance across the ocean,
     leaving me with the yearning, to hold on

His kiss on the tip of my ear, genuine,
     careful determination in showing love to
     the most vulnerable part of me

The ocean, the salt air, standing in the wispy
     tall grasses of the dunes,
     taking in the rare shared moment

On the train back, not speaking,
     absorbing the thoughtfulness
     One last hug before emails,
     lasting over a year

The emails, the excitement every week,
     the smiles, remembering the
     thoughtfulness in his eyes, speech

Cherished by his continued ardor,
     willingness to see me as I am,
     embracing my vulnerability

Only him, by whom I ever felt this honored,
        respected
        as a man should show a woman

Nuchtere realiteit,
        the ocean too big to hold on to the love,
        with unwanted courage,
                        I let my Dutch gentleman go

Billy Graham | 2000 Amsterdam

*Several of us from Lakeview Baptist Church
went to the Netherlands for three weeks to serve at
the nine-day multinational conference for preaching
evangelists*

*10,287 evangelists and other participants
representing 209 nations & territories*

nuchtere realiteit = sobering reality

Pen pals, not phone calls
before

Pen pals, better than long distance phone calls
        racking up those phone bills

Way before smartphones, even the internet
Way before generative artificial intelligence

Pen pals, not phone calls

Reading the words intended for me
Practicing communication through writing
Weaving together words
        to connect with the other person
Wanting to build a stronger bond

Stamped envelopes marking the date,
        Saving the envelope to protect
        the written shared thoughts

A gift in written words, a gift in long emails
        the thought, the effort, the time
                                rare nowadays
        more treasured than ever

Pen pals, not phone calls

Connection through words,
Listening to the voice behind the words
Paying attention to the nuances
Lingering thoughts
while writing a response

Keeping the written conversation going,
Further building the bond

Pen pals, not phone calls

Oleta
before

Mrs. Oleta Parker, an unusual bond, forged
through writing letters

On our white-columned porch,
unexpected appearance
        of my grandfather's wartime girlfriend,
not together long, strong yearning
        to find out about his family,
        his namesake son,
        the granddaughter who never knew
        the late Grady Junior.

Unusual bond formed through letters,
        stemming from Oleta's intuition,
when I wrote a long letter,
        a thank you for gifting me
        with her memories of my grandfather,
willing to share pieces of my life
        as a Moreman for her

Eager anticipation for her letters
Filled with handwritten stories about WWII,
savored the tidbits of information about the
grandfather I had heard about,
but never got to meet.

A mentor, bonus grandmother from Mississippi
Sparkly personality lacing through her language
Teaching me about life outside of Alabama
The taxicabs in NYC, her offer to send money

when I visit NYC
The gifts as part of her correspondence
Being there for my high school graduation

Until one day, a letter came from her daughter,
        informing me of Oleta's passing

Bereft sadness about no longer sharing written
memories,
        about being in touch with someone
        who knew my grandfather
        other than family

Since then, I visited NYC, taking taxi cabs,
thinking of Oleta

Honoring Veterans Day

*My grandfather, Henry Grady Moreman Jr....he
flew B-24s during WWII. I would have loved
listening to him share what he had been through.*

*Other than my flesh-and-blood relatives sharing
stories about my grandfather, Oleta was the one
who showed me who my grandfather was during
WWII, since she dated him during that time
when she was fifteen.*

*Oleta Parker has been a grandmother figure to
me after she reached out to us, asking if she
could get to know us. Since that first visit, Oleta*

96

*and I wrote each other letters until her daughter
sent me a letter to let me know she passed away.
I grieved Oleta and our letter-writing bond.*

*To emphasize how much Oleta meant to me, she
came to my high school graduation.*

*Through her letters, I grew to understand why
and how my grandfather and countless others
served in the military: to serve our country, to
defend our freedom.*

*To this day, I hold onto Oleta's letters as my
connection to my grandfather's bravery and
selfless service during WWII.*

*I also listened to my father and many others
recount their own services to our nation. Each
time I listened, my appreciation, admiration,
understanding, and respect grew more.*

*For each and every veteran, thank you for your
incomparable bravery, sacrifice, and valor in
serving our country, in fighting for our
independence, in esteeming others above self.*

friday nights
before

high school football games
friday night lights

fifth quarter
feeling left out

internet barely existent
smartphones unheard of

pizza, pepperoni
family gatherings

not going to the creek
not going to walk across the fire

books, engage
stories, immerse

rest after a week full of concentrated listening
solitude welcome

the quiet
no urge to pay attention, to understand

only disturbance
flapping sound of pages fanning open

**crawling up the blue-painted
concrete block wall**
before

me as one of the only two seniors finishing out
required credit of physical education before
graduation

jumping jacks and running one-mile runs
with lowerclassmen, mostly freshmen

after changing in the locker rooms, standing on
the polished gym floor, waiting for the bell to
ring,

one freshman asking a question, and it was the
first day of the school year, i spoke a few words
in response

he jumped, scrambled up the concrete block wall
painted in shiny Auburn High blue, startling me

      "Are you okay?" I asked.

      His eyes bulged more,
      his arms sticking to the wall,
      a wary spider

      "Are you okay?" I repeated, a bit slower.

      He squirmed higher up the painted
concrete block

I took a breath, willing down the
growing heat of embarrassment from my
cheeks and chest

the bell rang, and i gave him an uncertain stare
before walking away,
	noticing how he started
	slipping down the painted concrete
	block wall

	…after that strange crawl up the wall,
	he acted as a bodyguard
	for the rest of the school year,
	making sure that others treated me well.

not fluent
before and after

sign language, a foreign concept
to me

not fluent

i could not understand when someone
signs to me, only the rudimentary

not fluent

sign language, not how
i communicate, only the alphabet if necessary

not fluent

lipreading while using my residual hearing
is how i process, and i speak

      "You must get that all the time"
      then still press by asking if i could do
      something with sign language

not fluent

when a hearing person signs to me,
deflated

…my efforts in speech therapy, lipreading, speaking, reading, with having gone through a life-changing surgery are not being acknowledged

…signing to me signals that I am a category, not an individual

…the individual approach matters

**the most beautiful voice
in the world**
before

first date

first thing he said,
        "You have the most beautiful voice
        in the world."

me?

                his descriptions,
                awe on his face,
                drawing me in,
                opening up my heart

first time anybody has ever said that
no other man ever said that
        only him,
        calla lilies, white unity shared
        calla lilies, petals ripped
        calla lilies, ceramic shattered
        calla lilies, metal forged
        forgiven before calla lilies reclaimed
        calla lilies, blessed

Still pondering the first thing he said,
        "You have the most beautiful voice
        in the world."

parallel of distinction
before

what is it about a singer
that drew crowds,
that sold albums?

> The singer's voice,
> he said, closing his eyes

for flair

how can one singer be different
from another, if not for the type of music?

> See it this way,
> you love books.

At my nod,

> he continued,

> It is not the genre

> The voice is the

author's writing style

> The voice of a singer is

the unique part

> cannot be replicated

....

writing style, voice expressed
singer's voice, distinguished

parallel of distinction,
                    his way of connecting
                    with me

                    to communicate,
                    to help me see

The Freedom Tour 2016
before

"What is this Freedom Tour you're doing?"
the question asked over and over again
throughout the year of 2016.

"To reconnect with friends and family,"
I usually replied.
      "Also to find myself again."

This Freedom Tour exactly needed.

Originally, visit my sister and her family in
California
      …decided to combine two trips into one
(Las Vegas and Cali)
experience Las Vegas for the first time with Jane
      that two-in-one trip, found some
      missing pieces of my old self.

This epiphany, a reminder
of my long-ago desire to travel.

more I traveled,
      motorcycle-riding, paddle-boarding,
      mud-riding in ATVs, road-tripping,
      taking the train, petting all kinds of
      animals ranging from kittens and chicks
      to geckos and snakes, riding a horse,
      learning how to two-step, mountain
      hiking, painting, public speaking…

after each trip, found more pieces
            of the old Sarah.

began to look outward
of my inner world to find more pieces,
            found more answers about myself.

This Freedom Tour
            an investment in finding the new,
            stronger Sarah—***now Sarah Elizabeth***
            filled with peace and joy.

Throughout the Freedom Tour
with each trip completely different
from the last one,
the constant was the growth
of my relationship with the Lord.

Each trip revealed more of God's purpose
for this new chapter of my life.

Still......this Freedom Tour was not about only
me.

Friends and family whom I had not seen for
over a decade or two reached out to me,
inviting me to go visit them.

Thankful for each friend and relative
for having taken part in this Freedom Tour with
me
            –to show me their own world,
            to share their wisdom and love.

I pray that my visits have benefited
these wonderful people as much
as they have taught and loved me.

Without these people and their welcoming arms,
this Freedom Tour might not happen.

Freedom Tour 2016

*"Out of my distress I called on the Lord; the
Lord answered me and set me free"
- Psalm 118:5*

*"Now the Lord is the Spirit, and where the Spirit
of the Lord is, there is freedom"
- 2 Corinthians 3:17*

***Below is a list of the major destinations and
VIPs that made up this Freedom Tour 2016:***

*LAS VEGAS/CALIFORNIA, by plane
March 25-29 (Hebrews 11)
Jane Bruce and Hunter Bruce
Josie & Luke Stamps with their children, Jack,
Claire, Henry, and George*

WYOMING, by vehicle
April 30-May 17 (Hebrews 12)
Erica & Eric Patterson, Katie Brooks, Joe
Malek, Allie Bone, Alex Bone, Tyler Hitshew,
Bre Stroudt, Amy Bone, Richard Bone, Ronnie &
Becky Brooks

PASSED DISSERTATION DEFENSE,
Tuscaloosa
May 25 (Psalm 37)
Alison Lee Claunch, Dr. Claire Major, Dr. Erin
Naugher Gilchrist, Dr. David Hardy, Dr. Karri
Holley, Dr. Alan Webb

MEMPHIS, by vehicle
June 9-13 (Proverbs 20:5)
Kristin & Matt Horlings with their children,
Daniel, William, and Lucy
Jim & Nancy Etter

LOWER ALABAMA (Red Level/Opp), by vehicle
June 18-22 (Isaiah 44:21-23)
The Grantham Family Reunion
Heather & Jeremy Newman with their children
Jordan, Dawson, Elizabeth, Nathan, Abigail,
and Jeremiah

LAKES WEDOWEE & MARTIN, by vehicle
July 3-4 (Ezekial 31:4-9)
Jan & Woody Conger, Benjamin & Jackie
Blanton, Gale & Ben Adair
The Lundells and Sarah Dunn

DOCTORAL GRADUATION, Tuscaloosa
August 6 (Proverbs 19:21)
My intermediate family

SOUTH CAROLINA, by vehicle
August 19-21 (Micah 6:4)
Bethani Ford Smith
Jessica Wong & Brad Adcock
Aunt Lily

BOSTON, by plane
September 1-6 (Proverbs 27:17)
Beth and Josh Garver

PORTLAND, OREGON, by plane
September 21-26 (Habakkuk 3:19a)
Brooke Weber
Joan Lundell
Kathryn & Ash Taplin with their children Ella
and Oliver

LOWER ALABAMA, part II & III, by vehicle
October 20-22, November 6-9 (Ephesians 2:8-9)
celebrating Aunt Inez's life with Granthams and
all original Moremans
Heather & Jeremy Newman with their children

HOUSTON/MISSISSIPPI, by vehicle
November 15-22 (Jeremiah 29:10b-13)
Brad & Gina Moreman with their children,
Addie, Lucy, and Jacob
Matthew Mullins
Susan & Brent Kaziny with their daughter Olive
and Susan's mother, Mei Jang

Leslie & Charlie Patout with their children,
Charles, William, Henry, and Margaret
Mary Lynn & Randy Hotz
Andersson Dyke

NYC/NEW JERSEY, by Amtrak train & by plane
December 1-5 (Jeremiah 6:16a)
Brian Racelis
Christina Liu and her Brian Konsko
Ann Catherine & Cleve Haralson
Julie McCormick Veal
Tracey Lynn Snyder

GEORGIA/SOUTH CAROLINA, by vehicle
December 20-22 (Proverbs 31)
Lesley & Marsh Letson with their children
Murphy, Jack, and Eli
Jessica Wong & Brad Adcock

...and many, many mini road trips to Auburn,
Atlanta, Tuscaloosa, the lakes, etc.
I appreciate Jennifer Michaels Chambliss,
Laura Lloyd, Mary Stubenberg Hager, Kim
Gilchrist Hood, Tara Fulford, Pam Brasher,
Abby Brasher, Jonathan Joiner, Tena King,
Kristi Henson Chappell, Jennifer Ford Glaze,
Stacey Williams Foster, and the Pattersons so
much because of their willingness to fight for
me. Not to mention the hometown love from Kate
& Caleb Petty, rest of the family, Trina & Dan
Crowdus, Amy McKemie Dillard, June Fowler,
etc.

*...and let's not forget BIRMINGHAM (BHM).
Bahia Lukima, Sunny Graydon, Simone Wages
Engell, Adeel Amin, Sam Shouse, Krystal Pino,
Jill Cornelius, Bill Scott, Evan Thomas, Emily &
Bobby Herrington, Andi Bullard, John Newman,
Anthony & Alesha Oni, the Crawfords, Greg &
Dede Wood, Susanna & David Brown, Bart &
Leslie Box, Tyler Peterson, Lisa Kerr, Monique
Hahn, Stacey Nicole Godbee, Nik Jindal, Marlin
W., and the list keeps growing....*

*...and I am very blessed to be well-loved and
supported. Thanks to every single one of you
who reads this. Hopefully, this Freedom Tour
has taught you something, has given you
something to think about, has given you insight
about life.*

Love as a verb
before and after

True love is sacrifice.

Love is not what
another person can do for you.

> *JFK's "ask not what your country can
> do for you, ask what you can do for your
> country"
> resonated with what I am trying to say
> here.*

Love is not about you
and your own pleasure.

Love is not about
instant gratification.

Love is not a sprint; love is a marathon.
> ****And I am running the half-marathon
> tomorrow,*
>
> *therefore I know half of what a
> marathon feels like.*

Love is not simply a noun, but rather, more
powerfully, a verb.

Love is taking risks
such as willing to cook
for the other person when we hate to cook,

potentially become sick
while taking care of the other person
having the flu,

take a bullet intended
for the other person, and
accept the other person as is.

Love is not fear…
        love is bold courage
        to not accept lies and
        instead stand up for what is true and
        right.

Love is even about losing
the other person through constructive criticism,
        when we gently and patiently confront
        the lies
        and yet lose that person anyway.

Love should not be a cage
        with security cameras and control;

Love is freedom to trust
and enjoy each other
        during the ups and downs
        of what we call life.

While I had already experienced
giving my all to a person,
I knew that I can only experience true, agape
love through the Almighty One who truly
understands me.

Only He can fulfill me.

Only He can give me complete contentment
and joy.

I know that I cannot find such completeness
in another human being.

However, it is possible to have agape love
between human beings.

Agape love is unconditional.
        And I saw and still see this true, agape
        love in my family and friends' actions.

My own parents strongly believed in raising me
with the best possible education and upbringing.
        That meant not sending me to a deaf
        school,
        because they want me to grow up being
        part of the family.

My parents fought for me to be mainstreamed
in public education systems,
Vaughn Road Elementary in Montgomery
and their own alma mater of Auburn City
Schools.
        They endured criticism and negativity
        from numerous other parents of the
        deaf;
        my mother was told that she would put
        me in a very disadvantaged position,
        being awkwardly caught between two
        worlds.

Yet, my mother and father persisted.

Their persistence motivated me
in wanting to share with others,
help others overcome their own obstacles.

For eight years, my cousin Kate Daisy, MyBaby
keeps the memory of her Baby Eliza alive
        by fighting for a mother's right
        to have midwifery birth care
        in the state of Alabama.

When Kate was pregnant with Eliza,
it was the smoothest pregnancy.
        As of July 27, 2015, Eliza was born
        and lived for a few hours before passing
        away.

Kate is still determined to make sure
that her other daughters AdaRee and SarahJo
and other mothers-to-be have the right to have
birth with a midwife present.

She had been going to Montgomery
for Alabama Birth Coalition's rally
        to pass the Childbirth Freedom Act,
        allowing midwifery care to be practiced
        in Alabama.

For nine exact years, one of my best friends,
Jane Bruce, fought for her firstborn daughter
Hope's life.

At age fourteen in July 2009,
Hope had a cerebral hemorrhage
that led to immobile and neurological
issues.

Yet Jane did not give up,
because she chose love every day to
keep Hope alive

until God took her home in 2018 at the
age of 23.

Therefore....
agape love is not exactly romance,
but a whole lot better.

Several kinds of love
...and agape (unconditional) love is the best of
all.

Agape love equals forgiveness.
I choose to forgive
and let things go.

There have been people who hurt me,
but I choose to forgive.

Life is too short
to not forgive.

And I know I have done and said things
that hurt others,
and I pray they forgive me as well.

With love being messy,
      to forgive and to be forgiven
      is the best love anyone can and does
      have.

The Bible is the greatest love story of all.

A relationship does not guarantee
happiness or identity or even love.

Relationship does not equal love.

Love belongs to each and every person.

Love is a verb, *not only* a noun.

Listening to students' writings
after

taking a break from grading research papers
climbing out of this mindset
          numbed by reading students' words
          about how social media causes
          depression, isolation, and suicide among
          young adults and teenagers.

seeing posts of friends and acquaintances that
convey the same.

heart hurting while reading others' pain
from the distance and on the other side of the
screen

sharing words with anyone who is hurting
these words may be received as platitudinal and
insincere

careful with communicating with others.
shut down when my mind goes blank when
trying to comfort others

only S•H•O•W instead of tell—as my wonderful
English professor, Dr. Judy Troy, kept drilling
into me throughout four classes I took under her
tutelage at Auburn.

creative in communication strategies, including
social media.

ironically – THANKFUL for
the social media,

a substitute phone to talk with
others

cannot talk on the phone;
therefore, thanks to the social
media,
I grew and thrived
exponentially
in keeping touch
with others.

I still do.

disheartened how the society as whole
does not lift its head up from the smartphone
to interact with others in real life.

Lift the fog of negativity by lifting up your head.
Lift your head and look around.
Lift your head and see the beauty of the world,
both nature and man-made.
Lift your head and put away that smartphone.

The smartphone should be used only to connect
and communicate like a virtual phone,
not a substitute for LIVING LIFE.

look at the frown on my face
when I look down at my phone…
I would rather look up, smile, and
shout in joy for being alive.

Breathing alone is a gift.

Being able to communicate in any form is a gift.

Lift your head up and smile.

Sunday, 13 December 2020

Fall Term 2020,
pandemic-driven remote teaching and learning
Jefferson State Community College

#CreativeCommunicationsConsultant
#CCC
#create
#communicate
#consult
#speakerSEM
#SEMspeaker
#maestrospeaker
#differentlyabled
#ApproachFormula

a professor's heart
after

I would do anything to make sure that my students get the most out of their own learning experiences.
·

I know that having me as their teacher can be challenging at times, even stressful...because I would not go easy on them when it comes to writing practice.
·

I wanted them to see how writing is a powerful way to express their voices.
·

I shared my relevant experiences with them, so they would learn and not make the same mistakes that I stupidly made.
·

With a nod to the [Make It Stick] book recommended by my soul sister, I do not take lightly how my pedagogical methods can be unusual.
·

These methods help foster my competence as a college English teacher. My pedagogy is part of who I am, part of my speaking platform.
·

Looking back on my twenty-plus combined years of teaching, I am still humbled with how others believed in me, knowing that I would do the best of my own ability to reach out to the students in any way I can.

•

The students are *the why* I would get up at three in the morning to make sure the PowerPoints address the learning objectives for each class.

•

The students are *the why* I am willing to be open about my faults for the purpose of them learning from my genuineness.

•

And, I learn from them through their written, typed, and spoken words. They keep me humble...yet fun.

•

The students are *the why* I look forward to sharing my speaking platform. Without them, I would not be where I am.

•

The students are *the how* I am as an adjunct English professor.

•

Therefore, the students have my heart.

Southern Lady of Beauty
after

*Last week before the snow fell across Alabama
and in Auburn, I drove down from Birmingham
to share a few more moments with my beautiful
Gran. After parking my Darth Vader at Bethany
House, I first put on mascara. I must look my
best for the one who always exclaimed over my
appearance, especially high heels. In fact, I
brought a "bouquet" of high heels to show her.
The second I laid my eyes upon Gran, the
pointless mascara streamed down my cheeks.
The high heels were never brought out to wow
her. The next few days were spent at her side,
listening to her uneven breathing and
morphine-induced demands for water or "up,
up" to be moved for comfort.*

*Once, I read out loud my script for the TEDx
talk, my voice shaky with the reality that she
might not make it to see me, or at least watch the
video of me, on that red dot.*

*Although reluctantly leaving her side for work
and teaching for a couple of days, I felt cried
out. Even when she finally went home to be with
the Lord, I was relieved for her no longer feeling
the years-long pain.*

*Yesterday at the memorial service, I fooled
myself into thinking I would not cry again,
wearing just-in-case waterproof mascara. When*

*I stepped up to the podium to share the poem I
had quickly composed the night before, emotions
swept over me, making me struggle for several
seconds. Brother Al came to stand next to me for
comfort. I mentally pushed myself to look at the
microphone, to see its wire-meshed texture. After
taking a deep breath, I gazed out at the family
and friends of my grandmother before speaking.*

———————————

Sara Emma Jeanette, lady of beauty
The epitome of Southern grace

With her exclamations of how beautiful others
are
    "Well I declare
    Oh how beautiful you are!"

Through this Southern lady of beauty
    We have learned how to respect others
    Through the way we dress and carry
    ourselves

    "Well I declare
    Oh how beautiful you are!"

"Oh Lord have mercy!" whenever
    we share something with her
        ...that distinctive laughter
Before clapping hands together,
saying again, "Oh Lord have mercy!"

Her life, full of exclamations

Giving us love when listening to her
        "Well I declare
        Oh how beautiful you are!"

Sara Emma Jeanette, Southern lady of beauty

January 2018 – two months before the TEDx talk

Gran
Sara Emma Jeanette Abrams Brubaker
11 October 1924 – 18 January 2018

{ dis } connection
after

vision of a heartache
from the hope being deferred,
for not knowing how to remove the { dis- }
from the excruciating word, disconnection
.

.

.

the loss of my grandmother, Gran
what this Thanksgiving would mean without her

remembering the questions she asked me
such as why people act the way they do,
as if I had any answers

could only be silent
listen to her expressed declarations,
occasional feelings of loneliness

growing up a bit too quickly inside my head
having to acknowledge the sad reality about life
.

.

.

Why do we feel lonely and misunderstood from
time to time?

Why do we insist on having our way to the point
of exhaustion that all we could do is to drag our
scarred knees back to the One
...who can fulfill us

...who supplies all our needs according to the
riches of the glory of our Christ the King
...who fills this void that only He can and no
other human being can?

.

.

.

We are created to worship Him,
yet we chose to worship anything and everything
but Him.

We are weak in the flesh,
even though our spirits are willing.

We only trust what we can see and touch,
but not have faith in the unseen.

If only we could be silent and listen,
then we will hear and absorb the whispers from
the Almighty One
…who is the Lover of our souls.

He created us to *choose* to love Him or not.

He does not *make* us love Him.

When we do, we cannot help but love others
from the outpouring of our hearts in love with
God.

.

.

.

Only God can fill me with the love that I show
others, no matter how they treated me.

How can I not forgive and love?
I simply cannot stop loving and forgiving.

I want to yell or burst into tears of frustration
when others do not believe my genuine caring
and forgiveness for them
...that they choose to disconnect from me
            because I am too much, too nice
...I want to give up
...but I do not know how to not love and forgive.

Love and forgiveness are buried too deep within
me by the Holy Spirit that I can only endure the
excruciating pain others leave behind whether
intentionally or not intentionally.

What can I do?

I pray for healing while continuing to forgive
and love. I choose to be thankful that God uses
me for whatever purposes He has for my life and
the spiritual gifts He has instilled within me.

I give thanks to God for every person in my life
I give thanks for reaching this point in my life

Sunday, 18 November 2018
Two days short of the one-year anniversary
of my cochlear implant surgery

rough draft revised
before and after

what flows out, seeing it done
not wanting to go back and redo

not stopping to check for cadence of sound
not stopping to check for details

done, done, and done

ceramics, painting, kiln it
dancing, get through warm-ups
yearbook layout designed, photos cropped

not wanting to be held down
with expectations, ingrained sense
synaptic plasticity

hearing aids, rough draft
not wanting to revise the sound

hearing well enough

not so by regular standards

revisions necessary
communication flow better

grudges, changes as inevitable
black-and-white photo of the right ear
without a caption
the night before the surgery

another black-and-white photo
a silver candlestick formidable
against a stormy, cloudy night sky

leaving the skybox
overlooking the Regions field

red construction paper folded
in half, with niece and nephews' scrawl
"Aunt Sarah, we love you."

anesthesia, vulnerability
pulling me deeper into the rain of November—
rain of unexpected, a blur
splashing with blessings, sternum
tapped back to consciousness

rough draft revised
waiting for the red inked activation

paralleling with the script
readied for March

congruence, feedback
connection, synaptic

revised, more expectation

white noise revelation
after

nestled into burnt orange cushions,
an evening to relax
after intense auditory-verbal session.

cacophony, or is it a symphony?
not letting my senses ease.

"How could you stand it?"
      my neck tight, my eyes searching
      beyond the screen of the porch.

"Crickets, frogs, the usual,"
      her response.

"I do not know how you regulars
can concentrate in this noise,
      —what a nightmare."

"It's white noise,
you learn to tune it out,"
      she laughs.

"How? What's the point of
having hearing
          if
            you
               tune things out?"

drums, reverberating rhythm
before…and after

brother's drums in the attic,
the roof open to the night sky,
the pulsating illuminators of stars
matching metallic beats
      the iridescence of drumsticks,
      their aerodynamic
      hummingbird-winging hum
the wood support beams
framing the shimmering blue of the drumset
Hank in the groove, booming out the rhythm

      my sixth-grade speech therapist
      beats and rhythms, emphasis
      crucial framework for proper
      pronunciation

other siblings strong in music, singing
trumpet, baritone, trombone, tuba

      tenor saxophone, cheerleading,
      drum major of dreams
      snared staccato, crescendo
          —decrescendo instead
              into ease, control

reverberating rhythm
      in the car, any vehicle,
      only hearing the ups and downs
      of melody, distinguishing between
             wind, string, and drums

clang it all, peal it
    gong resounded
once activated, euphoric, ecstasy
     sharpening the starlit
illumination
against the dark restful sky, no longer sleep
deprived

    jarrin' rhythm though
    filling up the attics, cars, and my brain
    my whole being ringing
     now rowing, drumbeat,
     slap back
exploring, foundational moments *before*
evolving, moments *after*
    finding that ghost note
    through layers multiple,
    patterns syncopated

Hank Moreman, brother

the Ambassador
after

My brother supported me
serving, an Ambassador
TEDxBirmingham 2018,
there for me behind the scenes
          when I rehearsed
          and subsequently gave my talk.

him there to take notes
others their feedback

Although in a hurry to get back home
after my focus group/dress rehearsal,
he made the time to sit down and debrief
what I needed to do for my talk.

He knew me too well to not let me
delve into what-ifs by reminding me
that I could do it through Christ
Who strengthens me.

Simply knowing I have such a brother
          being there for me
helped give me the boost of confidence
          I needed to step onto that red dot

...and not only the red dot,
but also in other battles I face in my own life.

In a true Moreman fashion, he listens

He always lets me vent
about having my way
before calming me down
with his loving reminders
that things will turn out okay
as long as I have faith.

January – March 2018

Brad Moreman, brother

Post—#DWTSMagicCity Response to Concerns

after

I received a barrage of questions and comments
about the judges not moving their masks for me
to lipread while on the stage
after Quinn and I performed for the
#DancingWithTheStarsOfTheMagicCity2020.

        I even had long conversations with
        friends and relatives regarding this
        matter.

        I realized that I need to address this
        concern.

        I take responsibility for this presumed
        oversight.

In the few weeks leading up to the big night, the
organizers of First Light's Dancing with the
Stars of Magic City 2020 took the initiative in
reaching out to me via email. They shared their
concerns about making sure I get the most out of
this exciting experience. Other than offering
clear masks for the judges to wear, they asked
how they could accommodate me.

Allow me to share something from the past to
give you an insight about my response to their
concerns and questions about how to
accommodate me.

In the summer of 1997, I participated in Lee County's Junior Miss pageant. My talent was a self-choreographed ballet dance to the lyrics of "Somewhere Out There" in *The American Tale* animated film. Since Paula Nix of Nix Dance Studios was the director of this pageant and also my dance teacher, I was comfortable, and she was familiar with how I did things to perform on the stage. Thus, no one thought to ask me what I needed for accommodations, including answering a question on the stage as part of the Poise and Composure category. The emcee Jerry Teel stepped close to me and let me read the question before I responded. By the end of that night, I was the winner of the Poise and Composure category, along with being the first runner-up.

With that long-ago on-stage experience in mind, I learned from the #DWTSMagicCity experience that being poised and composed was more important than disrupting the flow of things.

I am only ONE person, and I do not want to draw the focus away from the flow of things such as timing and what people are saying. I prefer for others surrounding me to enjoy themselves. I prefer to watch others have a good time, which is better than my trying to understand every single thing being said. In my own personal perspective (please, please do NOT take my words as representative of any other person with a disability), I cannot help but be cognizant of how my asking what is going on disrupts the flow of good conversation and laughter.

Over and over again, I have chosen the way that better accommodates others rather than myself. The reasons why are complex, and I have gone through enough circumstances and social situations to discern the flow of things and also the moments where I may need to disrupt.

I have learned over time that I would gain information or understand what was going on if I simply waited. Patience is a necessary virtue and skill for me in terms of communication, because I would glean insight later about what is going on.

> Sometimes, hindsight is better than the present or even foresight. Sometimes, I would choose the most difficult road of communication to see how I can still interact with others with such little or no context…as part of expanding my creative communications strategy.

Back to the pertinent matter being discussed—throughout the back and forth email conversations with the organizers of the #DWTSMagicCity, I consulted with them on individual and public needs in person and via livestream. There were still some technological aspects already in place that would not meet my consulted suggestions. I did tell them that I had tried clear masks and face shields in professional settings. The result was distortion of sound and lipreading. I did request for whoever was speaking to pull down his or her mask for me to lipread. Even though the judges would be sitting in the front row and six feet apart, they were too far away for me to lipread effectively. We discussed this during the dress rehearsal as well. The other option was to have my dance coach and teammate Quinn and emcee Will to relay or repeat what the judges said.

My exact words in response to the organizers' question: "Back in the pre-Covid days, I did not have nor requested accommodations when I attended live events. I simply enjoyed the experience of being there, to absorb the excitement and crowd energy. That means I am good with everyone wearing individually-preferred masks throughout the event."

Note that the judges wearing their masks are to convey a message that this fundraising event is about serving and thinking about others. Since the organizers did reach out to ask what I would need, *I chose to go with the flow of things.*

What I did not anticipate is how the audience, both in attendance and via livestream, would perceive this supposedly oversight. I did not anticipate how the public would react, and I was bombarded with text messages, comments, and emails about this supposedly oversight.

It was not an oversight at all, because the organizers did ask how they could accommodate me. I only wanted to make sure the event ran smoothly in a timely manner. I did not realize the combination of trying to speak while catching my breath after dancing, the play-by-ear questions, and the judges talking would instill within me a delayed regret that I did not speak up to ask them to slow down and allow me to ask Quinn or Will to repeat what they said. I take the responsibility for not disrupting the flow of things.

I am still learning how to expand my creative communications strategy, which includes disrupting the flow of things by speaking up and asking for clarity.

Tuesday, 13 October 2020

First Light's Dancing with the Stars of Magic City 2020

Will Lochamy, emcee and radio host
Quinn Barrett, choreographer and partner

*This piece reflects my individual choices and not representative of others who have a disability. As Creative Communications Consultant, I strongly believe in each individual with a disability having the prerogative to determine what accommodations to request.

#CreativeCommunicationsConsultant
#CCC
#create
#communicate
#consult
#speaker
#SEMspeaker
#speakerSEM
#differentlyabled
#differentlyabledspeaker
#DisabilityInclusion
#DisabilityAwareness
#prerogative

The dancer's soul
after

two weeks since the stage for #DWTSMagicCity
...and the dancer's soul within me remains fierce
and strong.

danced to the lyrics of Russ' "Losin' Control"
followed Quinn's lead,

people asked
how could I dance if I did not rely on the music
while performing on stage?

Rather than trusting my limited hearing and
unpredicted possible technical difficulties
during the live performance, I danced...
       from the soul within,
       from my heart,
       from memory,
       from understanding the lyrics.

my coach and teammate recognized
my efforts during our practices

Quinn explained on my behalf to the audience
he knew what to say that others could
understand,
...whereas I only said, *It took a lot of work.*

on the stage for the dress rehearsal and live
performance,
intense focus, choreography, and timing

keep up with Quinn
         ...that I TUNED OUT the music.

My whole life, friends and family saw me dance
...and still could not grasp how I could dance.

Their questions forced me to ponder
the differing perspectives and experiences
when it comes to actual, regular hearing of
music.

still struggle putting into words
prefer that friends or family bring me to a place
where I feel right to show them.

not a blaring loud club, even though the crowd
energy certainly helps

the space inspires the dancer within me
readily put aside inhibitions
dance my heart out.

countless times of stubbornly refusing to dance
reasons: fear of rejection, ridicule, or looking
stupid

If the dancer inside me feels strong, confident,
and (most importantly) treasured,
I will share.

shared some of my dancing
to help with a great cause,

supported First Light's mission in providing a
safe, nurturing place for women and children

understood the need for a physically, mentally,
emotionally safe place

...because I overcame and survived
by leaning on a strong support system here in
Birmingham

danced to show my appreciation

Thank you.

Wednesday, 21 October 2020

First Light's
Dancing with the Stars of Magic City 2020

Russ. "Losin' Control." There's Really a Wolf,
Columbia Records, 2017.

Quinn Barrett, choreographer and partner

10.10.2020: I took a break from social media the day
after the big night (Thursday, 8 October 2020), and
now I will share some thoughts about this
#DWTSMagicCity journey.
First of all...we as a community raised $97K even
during such disruptive times, surpassing last year's
$78K! This data alone made me feel glad I got to
help make that happen.

Other than dance practices and performance with Quinn, I expanded upon my platform as Creative Communications Consultant through utilizing my creative and social media skills.

Due to the society being restricted socially and economically, I determined that the public needed something fun to follow/see each day on social media, along with being informed about the purpose of First Light's Dancing with the Stars of the Magic City.

I could not have done what I did without Quinn as my coach and teammate. Quinn and I were on the same page from the start when it came to every step of this journey. We both wanted to relate to the audience, and we agreed to do a narrative through our contemporary ballet choreography. We did not want to focus on showing tough ballet techniques; rather, we wanted to connect with the audience...which is an extension of my platform on communication. We wanted our efforts to highlight the purpose of the Dancing with the Stars of the Magic City 2020 as a fundraising effort to uplift others.

Naturally, I had to put myself out there, to let the public watch me as an individual with hearing impairment. After the performance and while on stage with the Emcee Will Lochamy, I did not answer in detail about how I could learn the choreography—it was difficult for me to put my thoughts into a few short sentences while catching my breath...my real answer would require at least thirty minutes to explain that although I could hear the music, I could not while performing because I

*subconsciously tuned the music out so I could focus
on the choreography itself and follow Quinn's lead.*

*The vibrations did not matter. The melody and rhythm
did not matter when it came to my being aware of
when and where to move.*

*What mattered was that our moves and appearances
fit with the lyrics.*

*The heartbeat, memory, and following Quinn were
how I was able to perform as a dancer.*

*...I chose the hashtags of #SEQuinn and #SeeQuinn
as to EMPHASIZE "seeing Quinn" while I danced.*

*Other than my loved ones coming from far places to
support me in person, I felt like a winner because
Quinn and I achieved what we wanted: to RELATE
with the audience.*

*Therefore, Quinn and I were truly #sequins for
having sparkled on stage.*

*#TeamMoremanBarrett
#CreativeCommunicationsConsultant
#CCC #create #communicate #consult
#speaker #speakerSEM #SEMspeaker
#maestrospeaker
#differentlyabledspeaker #differentlyabled
#SayMoreDancing
#TeamMoremanBarrett
#SEQuinn #SeeQuinn #sequins
#SparkleOnStage
#Dancer #AlwaysADancer #DanceFromTheHeart
#SoulOfDancer #DancerSoul #SafePlace*

Dichotomy of the question:
Can you hear me now?
after

after the individual is activated,
do not ask that question:

    Can you hear me now?

sound perception,
an individualistic metacognitive struggle,

that question hyperbolizes the lack of sound
reception,

not recognizing the cognitive shift from few
frequencies to multiple

not necessarily centering on the core,
where the bionic replaces something

ask instead:
-   What have you been experiencing
lately? Any noticeable changes?
-   Would you share any kind of
progress or practices you have
made, so I can understand?
-   What are your thoughts?

to answer your question all the same,
my concept of hearing has changed
since taking the plunge,

i could hear beforehand
with the assistance of hearing aids,
which amplified the natural, albeit
residual, hearing

my concept of hearing
multi-layered, with two dominant layers:
      1.   Natural, albeit residual, hearing,
           amplified with hearing aid – ***left ear***
      2.   Computerized hearing, processed
           with cochlear implant – ***right ear***

Now,

I can hear you
in multiple ways
     – hearing devices, environment, attitude

     nevertheless…

     dichotomy of the question:

          Can you hear me now?

others would tell you otherwise,
a vast difference between *before and after*

no more yelling my name countless times
     before I finally turned around

fewer repetitions for clear communication

their observations, not mine

their observations, made me aware of how much more
      sound perception I am gaining after

their observations, made me aware of how much more
      clarity in my speech I am uttering

therefore…

their observations, a gauge of my bionic state
      futuristic in sound perception,
      advancing beyond the natural

their observations, watchfulness with expectations higher
      matching with my overachieving
      tendencies

mascara moment
after

after almost a decade and half
complete disconnect

reunited, now visiting
naturally stepping back in the friendship

she getting ready for her performance
me keeping her company

catching up over the long lost years
yet well-tuned to nuances

"Will you hand me the mascara?"
i handed her the mascara without thinking

      i froze before turning
      to face Annette,
      her stunned expression
      mirroring mine…

      i comprehended
      what she said
      without looking at her lips

we had not spoken in almost fifteen years,
my brain still knew her voice and understood…

Anna Chance Brown, friend

*Note: I still struggle with speech comprehension,
even though I can occasionally understand
some words without lipreading.*

not eroded, polished
after

little girl, raw, full of dazzling laughs and smiles
like the sun dancing off awakened water,
the sound boisterous, ricocheting,
not knowing or understanding
about one day far off in the future
that taking a plunge would happen
after the uncut rocks, erode into smooth
hardness, rebuffed by the harshness of life
       the rejections, tears, bitterness,
unforgiveness, anger, depression
       the waves pulling, shoving, suffocating
       keeping mouth shut to avoid drowning

the trapped sense of not being understood,
swallowed up in the swirling of waters,
noise distorted into roars of bewilderment

pulling up to lay across the sun-warmed polished
stone,
taking comfort in the Capstone that others
rejected
       reveling in the hope beyond
       expectations,
       wiping away waterlogged hair
       from my eyes,

       gazing into the promise of siblings,
       both original and improved,
       trusting and receiving the pebbles
       skipping in my direction,

the stone, softened, pliable, teachable,
strengthened, forgiving

polished

Gold Award of Gwen
before

"Guweeen!" I struggled saying her name.

"No. Gwen."

Sigh. Scrunching my nose,
pulling my eyebrows together,
and clenching my stomach muscles,
I kept trying to articulate Gwen's name right,
and Beth was helping me.

We were at Dean Road Elementary, and it was
Friday after school...which meant Girl Scouts.

Gwen overheard me
trying to pronounce her name correctly.
A gentle smile glowing up her face,
especially her big blue eyes,
she came over and comforted me,
telling me it was okay and
that however I said her name
would be great with her.

From that moment on,
I looked upon Gwen
as a genuine, loving friend.

She made sure that I knew
what was going on around us.

She made sure
that I was having a good time.

She always looked like
she loved talking with me.

Her smile and blue eyes softly lit up
every single time we were in a conversation,
and we had countless conversations
from when we were about nine
all the way through high school,
especially during Girl Scouts and

Dr. Diener's Alabama civics class.
Gwen sat in front of me in that class.
Greeting each other with a good morning,
talking

Dr. Diener walked around in front of her desk,
her gold shoes
wide, black-rimmed coke-bottled glasses,
announcing her presence.

The crazy times that only those of us
in Troop 178 would ever know and understood,
some of which I enjoyed
making Gwen laugh or startling her.

Thankful that the seven of us
made it all the way to the Gold Award
with Gwen's mother, Mrs. Pugh,
as our troop leader.

Even after high school
Even on our separate ways,
Mrs. Pugh brought us back together
several times for good old times and,
of course, pizza and Girl Scout cookies.

---

2 April 2023

Gwendolyn Pugh Crumpton
2 January 1980 – 22 March 2023

May Gwen, Mrs. Pugh, and the Troop 178
be always strong in our memories,
along with our Gold Award,
Amy, Beth, Carla, Jennifer, Sarah, & Virginia

ponderings about
the art of conversation...
after

Lately, I found myself immersed
in conversations about conversing with others.

I know what I want out of any conversation
...to listen, learn, and share.

When I engage, I do not simply listen
with my hearing devices and eyes.

I listen with my heart and body
while keeping my mouth closed
by quieting my mind,
       quieting the need to verbalize
       this opinion or that feeling.

I ignore the surroundings while focusing
on the other person talking,
       because whatever the other person is
          saying
             matters.

When I share thoughts, ideas, and
understanding,
       I watch for any clues to see if my input
       is well-received.

More often than not,
       I sense impatience.

While we live in a
        "breaking news"
        "three-second attention span"
society as my blonde warrioress aptly described,
        I still could not pinpoint
        what made me feel bereft
        in some conversations and
        not in others until a few nights ago.
        A particular video chat with a friend.
I brought up several points about
how our society as whole seems to
no longer value the art of conversation,
how more people do not open up
in fear of their words being used against them
later.

Felecia's felicitous response sparked
        within me a realization
        that the majority uses conversation
as a sport to exchange wits
in rapid-fire succession.

        I do not understand why
        people overly engage
in witty repartee and
not in good, heartfelt conversations
that can bring healing.

People need each other.

People need to feel belonged.

People need to slow down and pay attention to
gain that sense of belonging.

People need to give time, energy, assistance, and attention first before asking or being given anything.

> Therefore when I open up personally and professionally,
> I take the risk of my words and heart being twisted.
>
> I believe in being honest about who I am, and yet many others seem to discourage such openness.

Deflection and dismissal are the surefire ways to discourage bonding and healing for both parties.

> I am still learning the art of conversation
> and how it involves the entire physique
to bless another person by setting aside the self, the pride, and truly listen.

---

25 June 2023

Deborah Strawn
Felecia Young

#CreativeCommunicationsConsultant
#Listening
#Conversation

paddleboarding moment
after

It has been a long while,
gliding through the glassiness of the waters
feels like a steak knife slicing through smooth,
the sensation meant to be revered

Feeling the breeze caressing my skin as I pull
the paddle through the deep waters,
my gaze catching the biofilm-covered rock beds,
seeing the small schools of fish darting about as
shadowy wisps

Stretching my neck to let the muscle fibers
feel the tension ebbing away
as I let out deep breaths, closing my eyes
for a moment, balancing my feet on the
fiberglass

Pulling the paddle through the deep waters,
pulling the steak knife through my deep
thoughts, to feel the smoothness of letting go,
letting my thoughts darting about as shadowy
wisps

Pulling the paddle through the deep waters as
the lone dead tree appears,
my gaze drawn to its trunk deep down into the
abyss, feeling the pull of the mysterious
unknown

Yet pushing the paddle around the dead tree,
choosing to breathe and smile as I keep slicing
through the heavy waters of the world, gazing up
at the overcast clouds, looking at the bright blue

my ears, untouched yet soothed by the breeze,
silence punctured only by the soft splashes of
the paddle

The Rebecca to my Sarah
before and after

Josephine Paradise, Joan Rebecca, Josie Stamps

My Josie

when teenagers,
I woke her up one random night,
well into the morning,
whisper-enunciating her name

"Josie"

"Josie"

"Josie"

...the coolest name ever

she opened my door,
her eyes barely open,
quietly waiting for me to ask or say something

startled at her appearance,
because I was only sounding out her cool name,
not expecting her to hear me
thinking how blessed I am
to have her as my sister

Growing up, I was in awe of her
to the point of jealousy, because

she.
was and still is.
cool.

She is on point brain-wise
I am en pointe toe-wise

with two older brothers,
I prayed hard for an older sister
to whom I could look up

She is indeed my sister,
although younger and the baby,
the more mature one
and I am so proud of her

My voice of reason growing up
going through tumultuous times
willing patience, seeing me through
tears, seeing me through joys

What I have done as a sister,
What she has done as a sister

Well prepared to have five of her own
Willing patience, seeing the five through
their tears and joys, uplifting them,
Uplifting her husband with her gentle, quiet
spirit, pleasing the Lord

Unsung hero on the soccer field
back then, unsung hero on the home front
As she teaches Latin with my *Illiad*
and *Odyssey*

The unseen strength within
She can do all things through the One
Who strengthens her even more,
With a strong provider as her love

The unsung hero,
My dear sister
The unsung hero, my sis-hero

Josephine Paradise,
the Rebecca to my Sarah,
The Josie!

---

17 September 2023 and 2024
– combination of two birthday poems

Josie Moreman Stamps, sister

Peeling off fear
after

The velvety feel of African violet petals
Enshrouding me, laying on thick
As to curl up inside
Avoiding the shushes
The shushes
●

●

●

Shhhhh
Shush
Shock straight to the core,
The velvet of the African violets
The color of royalty
●

●

●

Unfurling, curling out
Piercing the purple
Peeling off the fear
Peeling off the the the
Shhhhhh
●

●

●

Smoothing up the velvet
The color of royalty
Pulling up Manolo Blahniks
Wrapping my skin
With metal calla lilies
Forged with determination

To shush those shushes

Smiling as feeling, the purpose
From the steel-let-toes
Jarring smooth each step
Smiling, letting my voice
Silence those shushes

The velvet, turned up-to gladness
And joy, shushes now shushed
Laughter, clap-ter, the stamp-ter of approval

Saturday, 9 September 2023

100th Alabama Writers Cooperative Conference 2023

*I created this poem the day after I participated
in the open mic evening*

#CreativeCommunicationsConsultant
#Poet
#Speaker
#ReclaimingCallaLilies
#Ready
#LetMeDoIt
#OpenMic
#ManoloBlahnik
#ShoeAddict
#CallaLilies
#AfricanViolets

poetically kicking off
my signature keynote...
after

Thank you, Junior League of Birmingham,
for this significant evening.

The words flowed.
My heart sang.
Mishaps happened, and I used them
As examples, my Pepsi moments
That I transformed into learning opportunities
And better communication strategies.
Freshness strong through humor.

The red
Yes, that red
Holding the red-inked pen high
Sharing the moments
When genuine-hearted
Shows in the handwritten
Yes, that red
The red

Whatchagonnadoo
Let's sing and watch how
The words flow
'Cause faith strong
Faith strong

Wearing red
To be bold, to be a rebel
To show the possible in the

I.M.p.o.s.s.i.b.l.e

Keep wearing those stilettos
The same ones that punctuated
The red dot years ago
Sharing my Pepsi moments
Yes, that red
Yes. That TED
The red
Wearing red
As I smile, my heart singing
In faith and humbleness.

Thank you and shall I speak many more
In the red.

Tuesday, 9 January 2024

Keynote speaker
Mic Drop Academy Fall 2023 - Certified

#Red
#RedDress
#Speaker
#KeynoteSpeaker
#JLB
#JLBDEItraining
#InclusiveAwareness
#CreativeCommunicationsConsultant
#TheApproachFormula
#SEMspeaker

All about the approach
after

art in the approach
no presumption, no assumption

attention determines approach
patience, rare standard

adjust to the other's needs
not about you

absorb the moment, revel
strengthen the bond

birthday reflection...
after

02.03.2024 — the year my Grammy turns 100 in October, and today I am purrfectly forty-four.
I am doubly blessed.

I woke up to birthday texts and rolled over to grab the much-anticipated nicely bound book I got for Christmas. It holds treasured memories of my Auburn-born-and-raised parents bound together. Reading their own words about how the histories of both families, full of faith intertwined to create four offspring, the third and first girl being me.

I am doubly blessed.

Truly I am ever since how this past year brought me wind-whistling sharp clarity about being content in each and every circumstance.

Although always creative with my communications strategy in reaching out to others, I am still learning to listen, to see others. What is new for me is finally giving myself permission to ease from being so extra by working excessively hard to prove my worth • finally listening to my siblings, rest of family, and friends by easing off from these self-inflicted expectations. I am choosing to focus more on being...as a child of God, of faith...

Being content
Being grateful
Being loving
Being focused on the eternal

I am thankful for many blessings, and most of all, the Auburn High Class of 1998. I pray that my fellow '98ers understand that I love them and would do anything for them, simply because. I run for Robert on behalf of all of us '98ers, not for myself. I am not a runner • I run for us '98ers in memory of our dear departed ones • Gwen, Robert, Demetrius, Cherri, Brandon, Mookie, and others. I pray that our efforts will show how phenomenally strong and close our class is together #CampbellStrong, because we simply meld into each other, appreciating each other simply for "being" • inspiring me to keep running and writing to share more of myself.

I write to understand
I write to love
I write to breathe
I write to uplift with hope

Looking up from typing all this, I smile at my double feline blessings as they look at me. Time to get up and feed the growing boy cats. Then treat myself to a double Pure Barre 🩶 🩶
Thank you for loving me, for showing me you care, for reading my words as part of my birthday.

Foreverrr and always
before and after

Ever since she stepped foot in the Glom office
A rare friend so fiercely loyal

Thankful for her
Keeping me in stitches with laughter
Making me look up from layouts and pages

Smiling with joy
Knowing she gets me
Could not imagine a get-together
Without talking about everrrrythang

I get her
We get each other
Through glom, sororities, War Eagles

Traveling yet still connected
No matter what
Connection forged stronger
As we experience more of life

We simply get each other

Reminding each other of strengths, talents
Being there for each other from Texas to
Alabama
And back and forth with drives and flights

Let's go to another SEC game
Let's stay up many more nights, jib-jabbering
our heads off

More pages please of treasured moments
More photos please of captured moments
Always

Thursday, 11 April 2024

Alana Fields Mardin
Forever friend, War Eagle Always and Forever

NettieAnne Margaret Petty

after

Walking up to the tent,
Listening to the preacher,
Listening to the chosen Scriptures,
Listening to AnnaSmith lead the singing

Holding my arms,
my eyes hidden behind shades
Staring out at the careless stream of cars
Roaring by and around the roundabout
Taking in the spires of the iron fence
The flags over graves, whipping in the wind

Looking up at the ancient centerpiece
A giant post oak, its shade
Seeping cold beneath my skin
The shade, scattered shadows of leaves
The post oak standing guard over generations
Of us, the Auburn Bradleys and Botsfords

Singing ended
Soft voices
Seeing more of family
Hugging, not saying anything
As we know words are not enough
Only The Word matters

NettieAnne is now gathered up in embrace
With her older siblings, especially Eliza
Who are already in heaven

Dark pink roses, the two sisters now share
As they reach for each other

As I hug MyBaby as we reach for each other
Being there for each other
With the winds storming around us
Whipping hair into our faces,
Hiding the brightness of the sun
No matter the hotness of the sun
Still cold with numbness
As we dig deeper for faith

True Alabama red mud
Perfectly dry to embrace a sweet soul
Bearing the historical significance
In her name, like her older sisters

AdaRee,
after Grammy and Nanny

Elizabeth Anne "Eliza"
after Katherine Elizabethanne, KateDaisy,
MyBaby

SarahJosephine, SarahJo,
me and my sister's namesake

NettieAnne Maragaret,
after Great Mama and Cousin Margaret

The winds,
pulling the longleaf pines and post oaks
Against pure blueness of the sky
Sun unfiltered, yet hair covering our faces
As to hide more of our emotions

Reaching for the loving arms of family,
Knowing that Eliza and others are pulling
NettieAnne into their arms
As the Lord lovingly looks over them
And us, like the ancient post oak

Lifting my face up, allowing the sun
To kiss away the cold shadows
'Tis peace in the Lord
that only we can keep going
While growing stronger in the family
With reminders letting us know
That faith prevails

Friday, 12 April 2024

NettieAnne Margaret Petty
Born asleep on Sunday, 7 April 2024

Sweetheart of a friend
Before and after

Hard to pull together many memories into a
poem that honors one of my best childhood
friends, Emily Sams Keown. Tears make it hard
for me to see what I am typing. Forgive me as I
alternate between present and past tenses while
typing this.

> When I received the news via text
> yesterday, my eyes filled up instantly as
> my heart squeezed tight. Sitting down
> hard, I put aside my own life's messes
> and absorbed the reality of Emily having
> passed away the day before.

Not wanting to stay home, I took a walk through
Railroad Park for the block party at Tasty Town
sending off the Birmingham-Southern College's
Baseball team for the DIII College World Series.
After a while, being surrounded by the
black-and-gold joviality,
> I could not stay.
> I left without ordering anything.
> I walked back across the park.

> On the way, I saw a neighbor.
Bob gave me sage wisdom that reminds me of
what Emily said to me at the bowling alley the
summer before we entered high school

...something along the lines of not
following the crowd
        ...being true to my own values.

She was with her brother Matt's group of friends,
and I was with my brother Brad's group of
friends.

        Emily loved me for exactly
        who I was and still am.
                Throughout high school,
                college, and
                our class reunions,
        I thought about 14-year-old Emily's
        words of wisdom and encouragement,
                which are mine to treasure in
                my heart and that I would not
                share with the world.

When I climbed up many flights of stairs to get
home, numbness and sadness grew in my heart
as I informed our fellow '98ers.

This morning after reading a fellow '98er
David's tribute to Emily and some Scriptures, I
wrote down the moments I have shared with her.

        We both are the third child in our
        respective four-children military
        families.

        She has this quality that captures the
        Mona Lisa essence.

She favors Rene Russo strongly.
She is beautiful, especially how she
emanates thoughtfulness from within.

It was that quality that caught my awareness
when she made her late entrance almost halfway
through our fourth-grade year at Dean Road.
Everyone wanted to know who this new
reddish-brown-haired girl was.
All the boys noticed.
We were only ten,
but the boys definitely were interested.

One night her older sister, Sarah, came over to
my house to study for a math test with my older
brother, Hank. Sarah smiled at me, "You know
my sister, Emily."

After that evening, I had to wait a long while
before all fourth graders got together. Emily was
in Mrs. Dillard's class, and I was in Mrs.
Swinney's class. During a tornado drill or
something when we lined the fourth-grade wing
hallways and huddled, I leaned over to Emily
and asked,

"Would you like to be friends?"
She nodded, cementing that bond that
only forever friends could understand.

The three of us—Emily Sams, Sara Olds, and me—were the three musketeers or amigos throughout Drake Middle (those bus rides) and AJHS years before Sara moved to Kentucky.

> Summer walks,
> sleepovers,
> stealing her mom's favorite Snickers,
> skittering down steep hills,
> shortcutting through the woods...

Emily, along with Beth, Carla, Jennifer, and Wendy, was in the framed photo of my 13th birthday. That framed picture sat on the nightstand next to my bed throughout high school and college before I moved out of my parents' house.

Emily was, and still is, one of the rare friends who truly accepted me—warts, idiosyncrasies, and all.

> She made sure I knew
> what was going on.
> She included me in conversations
> without making me feel
> like I was a burden.
> She loved me so well as a friend
> that I felt 100% normal around her.

Throughout high school and even after when we drifted apart, our bond always stayed the same whenever we saw each other.

When I heard that Sara passed away in 2002, my
first thought was of Emily. I jumped in my Jeep
Cherokee and drove to the Sams' house. I cried
in Mrs. Cindy's arms, asking for Emily since I
did not know how to reach her. We did not have
social media, and I did not have a cell phone at
the time.

Emily showed up for Sara's memorial service at
Lakeview Baptist, as I knew she would.

> We sat together,
> sniffling in our tissues,
> not saying a word,
> our hearts were woven tight together as
> we comforted each other.
>
> When the memorial service ended for
> Sara, Emily and I stood up.
> We looked at each other without saying
> a word before hugging for a long time.
>
> After quietly saying "I love you" to each
> other, I watched her walk across the
> church's grassy meadow to her car.
> I hold on to this memory to this day.

Emily was our Key Club Sweetheart, and she truly is the sweetheart among all '98ers.

She loved every one of us '98ers.
#AHS98ers

Emily Ann Sams Keown
27 April 1980, born in Vicenza, Italy
27 May 2024

Fourth Birthday
before

Saw the potential in me
Present in form of a microphone,
radio, and a headset system,
          as if she could see me on the stage

Saw the potential in me
Support in form of encouraging words,
questions, and prayers
          as if she could see me speak

Only four years old
and she knew what I needed—
          encouragement
          to express my voice

Not the presents themselves
rather seeing the potential
          supporting the expression
          of my voice

only four years old
          Grammy saw and knew
          that my voice must be expressed
          that I would be drawn to the stage

Friday, 3 February 1984

In Mom's handwriting: Sarah celebrated her fourth birthday for several days. Birthday breakfast became a tradition for our family this year because of busy schedules. Wearing a crown and choosing a favorite menu was part of it. Grammy couldn't wait 2 more days 'til her party to gift her a microphone, radio, headset system. Sunday afternoon we had her party. Teachers and friends were present—Linda Rubio, Pam Hughes, Deborah Strawn, Sue and Leslie Mossholder, Aunt Beth, Sasha, Kate, Richard, and even Uncle Pete, and of course, Aunt Glen were here for a Strawberry Shortcake birthday party! Clothes, puzzles, purses, and a very cuddly Teddy Bear were presents! Isn't it fun to rule the world—or at least your world for the day!

Forty-four years
after

       forty-four years shaped by family
       experience entrenched deep in the roots
       of oaks, magnolias, longleaf pines

sun glittering through the leaves
fog, a dreamlike haze
billowing around the bark

       the feel of mossy grass under bare feet
       the feel of wet cool blades of wild grass
       the feel of raspy pampas grass

the red mud holding long-held recipes
the red clay firming the baking
the red stone firing, smoking the meat

       cadence of vellum, a background
       caravan of vehicles, a reunion
       cacophony of ventilation, a declaration

nothing makes sense
yet everything does make sense

s e p a r a t I n g fle*shhh* from its wants
leaning closer into Him for guidance

       patience, a virtue, necessary
       contentment, a soothing presence

wait and see
answers will come
no need to dwell in questions
wait and see

    patience, refined
    contentment, family

music in the heart
melody in their voices
mine, still a mystery to my ears, bimodalistic,
multimodalistic

Windows, interruptions
after

series of interruptions, or disruptions
windows into our souls,
revealing the core of our beliefs
        patience, impatience
        contentment, discontentment
        love, indifference (not hate)

seeing through the glass, to the hearth,
        what keeps our fire going
        —family, friends, faith
        and, freedom. The freedom to be…

listening to each other reminiscing, windows
seeing through the glass, even if we cannot hear
        we still gain insight by listening,
        understanding beyond interruptions

Listening, seeing through the glass
seeking understanding, not getting angry
        at plans being changed, disrupting
        the ease of communication

Interruptions through drastic changes
        struggling to not give in to bitterness
        from the disruptive altering of sense,
        any sense

Others experiencing interruptions
        meeting doctors
        wearing hearing aids
        seeing through glasses, lenses

"Welcome to my world" stated with gentleness
        patience, rather than impatience
Look up and into the eyes of the other person
        Contentment, rather than discontentment
Wait, the answers will come
        Love, rather than indifference
Let go and hope beyond comprehension

Language in the movement,
in the expression,
in the regard

Genuine connection in communication
more than the standard

Sunday of *confrustrations*
after

Confronting uncertainty
      banished to the waiting room
      rest starved without the cacophony

Confronting uncertainty
Questions being addressed
      The doctor willing to share
      his own observations,

      he would not have done
      anything different,
      he would have done
      the same,
         same outcome

Confronting uncertainty
      my way of dealing with grief
      turning inward, asking questions
      wanting distraction,
Avoiding uncertainty

By confronting my mother
      about decisions
      about cochlear implant

Confronting reality
Slamming into frustration
confrontation + frustration
Sundays full of *confrustrations*
      wanting answers

Would things have been different
if I was born this year and not 1980?

       Would she and my father
       have done anything different?

My mother facing confrustrations
       Her Mama, my Grammy
       Her daughter, me

Her two sisters leaning in,
       sharing their own perspectives
       addressing my stubbornness
       of wanting to know

       Would she and my father
       have done anything different?

Who knows?
       Only absorbing
       the reality, the facts

Confronting my own stubbornness
       Insistence of gratitude

       Glad that I was not implanted
       when I was a baby
       Glad that I was the one
       to make the decision

Experiences my own, shaping my reality
       Yet slammed with others' realities
Their reasoning shaped by experiences, facts
       Research, societal landscape,

Consideration for family, communication, and
education
        Wanting the best outcome,
        shaping their decisions

Confronting that reasoning, that reality
        Insistence of gratitude

        Glad that I was not implanted younger
        Glad that I was the one to make the
decision
Experiences my own, shaping my reality
        My own *confrustrations*

However…the what-ifs…
        The timing, the research
        Would things have been better?

My heart aching, facing the unknown
        Stubbornness fading, unobscured
        Letting go of insistence
Accepting that loved ones focus
Best answers possible
To be together, not banished to the waiting room
To not lose focus on finding the best possible
answers.

Turn away those what-ifs
Absorb instead
the beauty of love, faith, and hope
Beyond of those time-wasting what-ifs…

Turn this Sunday of *confrustrations*
      into bringing together the truth of what
      truly matters

Once relaxed, the gift of nurses welcoming us
back in her room, to be with her

      our gratitude in form of silence,
      focusing on what matters,
      the best answer
           in being, not doing

Hospital waiting room, not in Grammy's room
Sunday, 1 September 2024

Understated understanding
after

Aunt Glen putting aside her Kindle,
giving me her undivided attention,
trained by the toddler, the three-year-old me,
        when I clasped my hands on her cheeks
        while she was stick-shift driving
        her brown 1983 Toyota Corolla

        forcing her to look at me,
                *"Look at me when I am
                talking to you"*

Away from the road, away from the Kindle,
        her stunning jade green eyes
        steady straight in mine

The relationship child as Grammy described
        Aunt Glen pinpointed the heart
        of my demands, of my questions,
        of my insistence of being seen

She responded to my wonderings about
        my parents' decision-making
        being aligned with the time
        and technological advances

*"...when I saw you in that audiologist's office,
how you kept asking for volume."*

She knew the depths beyond
         what I was asking for
         during the activation,
         back in December 2017

         and now, seven years later,
         in September 2024,
she saw that same depth beyond
         what I was asking for
         while we were waiting
         for answers

With that understated understanding, I felt seen.

Prevailing

after

Glenda Ree Grantham Bradley is with Jesus.

She drew her last breath last night (Thursday, 5 September 2024) in the hour of seven. She was surrounded by her four living children and some grandchildren.

I had my alone time with Grammy the evening of Wednesday, 4 September 2024, after several days of not knowing if I should go to the conference where I worked or stay by her side. I said my final goodbyes the next morning before leaving. When I arrived in Orange Beach and met with my cousins, one of whom is Grammy's nephew, I realized how God's will had shaped the plans I made. Being with Greg and Dede when I received Mom's text—"She's with Jesus"—brought me comfort. Though I had been frustrated by not having the conversations that I needed with Grammy, being with Greg gave me that sense of Grantham-ness I had been subconsciously seeking. Connecting with them felt like linking branches of the family, with traditions, beliefs, mannerisms, and shared understanding flowing through us, like sap from deep roots.

Below I changed my hastily scrawled September 3rd poem to emphasize IS:

High-heeled red roses of "whatevers"
grace filled with love and prayers
More time IS a gift...

Our concept of time is on this side of eternity,
and Grammy is now on the other side, which is
timeless and full of life.

What I, her granddaughter, have been struggling
with in the past several days is accepting that no
one has answers while we spent time with
Grammy. Tears as our makeup, tissues as our
jewelry, family stronger together as we looked to
each other, encouraging words and memories of
Grammy, willing for Grammy to hear us.

Grammy is truly a strength as a Grantham
when one says, "Grantham"
        ...it sounds and feels great
Great Grantham in our Grammy

With her fiery red-haired essence
        yet with quiet grace
Gentle greatness in her love, full of grace

Grammy is Grammy. Anyone who has ever met
her would feel grace. Being in her presence is
soothing. I am not saying that as her
granddaughter. She was, and still IS, truly an
embodiment of grace. To know her is to
experience grace in the most humanly, tangible
way, because she was steady in her words,
actions, and even thoughts to honor God.

"If the Lord wills it..." has been her steadfast response to whatever.

"Whatever" is her word to reflect the grace she so easily gave to anyone and everyone.

The conversations Grammy and I shared over that wooden table in her kitchen, the Bible and notebook covered with prayers in her gorgeous cursive writing, me leaning over with a mischievous glint in my eye as I tested her faith by asking outrageous questions and her responses were spiritually lined, even when she laughed at my boldness.

The conversations when I sought solace in her wisdom, especially about my two failed relationships. The last full conversation we had, which was a few months ago, she asked, and I responded, "I am better off."

She then knew I would be okay.

The morning after—Friday, 6 September 2024

the Grantham essence
after

Glenda Ree Grantham Bradley
        a gentle ginger spirit
grew up in Red Level,
        growing the garden of grace
        throughout her life,

rows of spiritual vegetables and fruits
patience, genuine thoughtfulness, goodness

simple gift of snapping beans
        agricultural fellowship, grit

weeding out warring harshness of trials
        with a bulwark of forgiveness
        with softly spoken "whatever"

framing with red roses of Truth, love, and hope
        most faithful in seeking the Lord
        steadfast in the Scriptures

Living life as an example,
        the standard of a godly woman,
        guiding others to the Lord's goodness

That Grantham essence
cultivated, mature in the Auburn soil

"If the Lord wills it..."
        her voice in reverence,
        her hands stretch out,
        a respectful blink of eyes

the heart of Farmville,
        hospitality, granting the home
        as a refuge for many

As the Lord wills it

Serving others, unconditional giving
        Others gravitating to Grammy's
        Countless many expressing gratitude
        for her generous welcome

That Grantham essence
        The element of greatness being the Lord
growth in faith, never ceasing
        vigilant in prayer, loving Jesus

Glenda Ree Grantham Bradley
legacy strong through grace

                    a life well-lived

Monday, 9 September 2024 Memorial Service Poem

Grammy
Glenda Ree Grantham Bradley
14 October 1924 – 5 September 2024

Poetry is part of me
after

Two cousins, two brothers
giving weight to honoring
and remembering the wisdom
of our beloved

Spoken words fading in the wind,
Yet acutely felt long after
Honoring and remembering the wisdom
Of our beloved

Vehicular flashes, their roars unnoticed
Ancient oaks steady
Blue tent giving shade
Rows of metal folding chairs before
the one to whom we are saying goodbye

Sun coating the gravestones
Grass well cut

One brother walking beside me,
his voice pulling my eyes
        to see what he is saying,

        "Why poetry?
        Were you asked to do it?
        Did you feel forced?

                Or, is it a part of you?"

I pause, giving thought to his questions.

"Poetry is part of me."

Without another word,
We walk away from the Farmville cemetery,
towards Grammy's where we would still feel her
in the heart pine,
in the kitchen,
in the family den

Where we know we will still grow,
honoring and remembering the wisdom
of our beloved

In her wisdom, she knew
That I would grow
        determined to have a voice
        expressed through words,
        through speaking,
        through mastering the *Sss*,
        through poetry…

A Butterfly To Be
before

The butterfly is in me, flitting
over the kaleidoscope of
flowers, unsure of which scented
petal to call my own. There is something
about each kind of flower that is
desirable to be near.

Happy as always, I would gladly envelope
myself with their inviting
faces, feeding myself with their
nectar of knowledge and excitement, I feel
content just for the moment.
Just for the moment long enough.

Subdued and restless at the same
time I may feel, my wings give me the
exhilarating thrill of seeking for more
honey from fresher ones. As a butterfly,
it is a blessing to be able to join or get
away, whenever is at the uppermost need.

With my fragility, it is surely a
curse by having my wings warily refraining
from danger. Never mind the admiring
glances at the designs on the wings, there's
the paranoia and awareness in order
to shield myself by gliding away.

What a relief to be able to abscond, and
flitter away to some clear pond, surrounded
by such breathtaking nature against the
marbled sky. 'Tis here where my
thoughts tumble out freely as I stare at
the reflecting smoothness of the water.

'Tis a meaningful gift from God that I am a
butterfly. My wings are of an unusual shade of
tawny gold with a greenish-blue shimmer. My
species is declared as rare. Such a word
is rare, indeed, I am my own and not part of
some named group according to typicality.

Craning my neck, I stretch effortlessly to move
my wings into the breeze. As I pass along, the
leaves sway in answer. The motion creates
music, to which my wings swoop into series of
graceful choreography to match with the
atmosphere of dreaminess and
peacefulness with childlike innocence.

---

*1997, when Sarah Elizabeth Moreman was seventeen
and in her senior year at Auburn High School*

Sharpness
after

Sharpness of each raindrop
       hitting the windshield
Sun shining stubbornly
       through the grayness

Sharpness of each flick
       of every light switch
My turning on like the light
       yet electrified

Sharpness in the clacking
       of ice
Glaring at the friend
       who grins at my wince

Sharpness of my new
       normal, which I originally
       did not want…

       yet got done anyway.

Spring Term 2018

A poem about cochlear implant

*Dr. Moreman created this poem as part of
teaching her students the elements of poetry
while encouraging them to write their own poems*

Seeing hope through the rainbows
after

mist hanging in the air, lingering
spectacular prismatic hope, oftentimes
a double blessing, the promise fulfilled
through the clearing of smoke
that emanated from the Sloss,
yet with the same forging magic,
making a better Birmingham

breathing in the crystallized air,
humid with the Southern heat, steaming
from the Morris cobblestones underneath my
high heels, bravely marching over
the round stones soaked with history,
unevenness, willing a face plant
to happen, for I have left behind the
worst of tears, for magic in the spectrum of hope
as floods of pain now evaporate

iron ore of friends,
limestone of foundation,
coal of faith
…transforming into magic
…magic transforming into an array of colors

the spectrum of hope,
…melded
…blended
…forged
into the architecture of the Rainbow Viaduct,
our beloved Richard Arrington Junior,

overseeing the parallels of railroad tracks
and cobblestones,
…history
…honor
…hope

the gateway of wonder,
the bridge of sunsets,
the rainbows of hope

Tuesday, 19 September 2023

*A poem created for An Evening of Poetry
at Juniper as part of my application for the
City of Birmingham's Inaugural Poet Laureate*

▼ {Connecting to Communicate} ▼ an
evening of poetry...

*Several weeks ago when I shared my endeavors
over the next few months while catching her up
on my met goals—especially the recently
published collection of {Reclaiming Calla
Lilies}, she enthusiastically encouraged me to
find a beautiful space and do an evening of
poetry, to share my story. I dedicate this evening
of poetry in her honor—thank you, Melvia
Walton.*

This evening would not have gone smoothly if it weren't for Brandon Rose and Felecia Young helping me prepare and set up. They listened to me practice quite a few times, their being there for me inspired me to speak louder and more confidently.

Krystal Pino, with her innate sense of sending me uplifting, constructive words, reminded me of how far I have come since our LIV Parkside days, how much I have healed over the span of several years. As always, she is with me in my heart as she travels the world.

Ryan Nelson, who has been there for every one of my big stage worthy moments including TEDxBirmingham, Dancing with the Stars of the Magic City, along with having helped me live in BHM and gifted me with the love of motorcycles, flew across the ocean from Lisbon in time to listen to me speak poetically.

Kimberly Harwell, thank you for being there for me, bringing optimism when I shared my concerns, reminding me of His goodness and grace.

I delighted in hugging and catching up with friends, including Casey Gamble and Jennifer Watts. I look forward to many more of these catchups, to hear about what is keeping them focused and busy these days. I loved it when Casey asked about what inspired me to write the {Reclaiming Calla Lilies} collection of poems.

*My heart was deeply touched when one of my
former students, Jaycie Mandrell, and her friend
Kaylee showed up. Seeing Jaycie there as I read
poems brought back memories of the class two
years ago. This particular class saw me go
through so much, deepening my appreciation for
each of them.*

*I was thrilled that my cousin Ben Crawford
surprised me. Having family is always nice, and
his being there represented my family that
sprawls all over the Deep South and more. And,
I am thankful for all of them.*

*The two days before this evening of poetry, my
stomach was tied in knots thanks to a flat tire
upsetting my carefully planned logistics.
However, I appreciate how Express Oil Change
and Enterprise aided in my transportation
needs, plus it is a nice feeling to have a new set
of tires!*

*Heartfelt gratitude for Carla Kelly Johnson.
Like Ryan, she was there for every one of my big
BHM moments. Our bond still strong after a few
decades, she understood me and I never needed
to explain myself to her.*

*Carla, Felecia, and Brandon sat with me for a
few hours afterwards, and our conversation
flowed as we enjoyed the gorgeous courtyard of
Juniper, with the Edison-style lightbulbs lighting
up as the sky deepened into dark blue hues
studded with stars.*

Thank you, Juniper Birmingham, for letting me flourish in your beautiful space with my creativity.

Then, I remembered how I was inspired to read poems out loud as part of my speech therapy. Thank you, PJS.

#CreativeCommunicationsConsultant
#Speaker
#CollegeEnglishTeacher
#AdjunctEnglishProfessor
#Poet
#Author
#ReclaimingCallaLilies
#CallaLilies
#Healing
#Ready
#OnTheMic
#AnEveningOfPoetry
#PoetryEvening

| Afterword |
Forging my voice and answering the calling of helping others find their voices

After December 2002 college graduation and ensuing holidays, I found myself weaving the old, but trusty hunter green Jeep Cherokee up the curves of the Shades Valley. It was evening, and Christmas lights were still twinkling everywhere. Easing the vehicle to a stop on the gravel circular driveway in front of my cousins' house, I then pulled my suitcase out. My cousins, Greg and Dede Wood, greeted me, welcoming me to Birmingham. The next six months set the foundation for my love for Birmingham as my curious heart drew me closer to downtown, my eyes searching for the magnificent sculpture of Vulcan. He was not there. I did not see him at all, only that I learned about this god of fire and forge from listening to my cousins.

When my internship at Oxmoor House Promotion within Southern Progress Corporation ended, I left to further my education back in my hometown of Auburn and subsequently marrying the one to whom I gave my first kiss.

> After the ink was dry on my divorce papers, the dissertation successfully defended, and graduating with a doctorate several months later, this cataclysmic change solidifies the third segment of my life, as I now go by Dr. Sarah Elizabeth Moreman rather than returning to simply Sarah Moreman after dropping my former married name.

It was not until January 2016 when I followed my curious heart to find Vulcan again. Having found the 56-foot-tall cast iron statue back on its pedestal, I also found my new home next to Railroad Park, where I absorbed the magic of giving back to the community through the fireworks over Regions Park that are designed to uplift the spirits of the precious ones at Children's of AL, through the recycled and sustainable materials throughout the park design, and volunteerism. I searched for opportunities to be part of this giving spirit that defines the growth of the city.

I delved into UAB Toastmasters, Birmingham Barons, TEDxBirmingham, and the Junior League of Birmingham (JLB). Through these involvements increased my awareness of how much Birmingham meant to me personally, professionally, and communally.

I found my voice, and the city of Birmingham welcomed me deeper into its folds of community. Through my efforts of giving back to the community, I seek ways of ensuring that others have a voice in varying ways of communication to find that genuine connection. While I help others, I learn from them. When I was going through the process as a speaker for TEDxBirmingham 2018 with my speaker coach Anne Wright Rygiel, I learned to tighten my focus, to provide clarity for my individualized way of giving back to the community—using frustration and miscommunication as learning opportunities to improve communication.

Pedaling back to my college days at Auburn University, I chose English as my major primarily to improve my communication skills. Under several English professors, especially Dr. Judy Troy, I thrived in creative writing to the point that I was advised to pursue poetry. Even younger as a teenager, I wrote poetry to use the beat and rhythm to learn how to pronounce words correctly. My speech therapist Mrs. Edith Jones, when I was in sixth grade, suggested that I try out for cheerleading. I already was taking dance classes for ballet, tap, jazz, modern, and

lyric. *Why cheerleading?* I asked Mrs. Edith.
She explained that cheerleading would help
instill within me an understanding about beat
and rhythm, that I must keep up with others
when cheering out chants. With mentors nudging
me to delve further into the art of language, I
wrote journals. The more I wrote, the more I
found my voice—especially after over a decade
of silence due to being told how others could not
understand me and that I did not have anything
worth saying for others to hear. *The irony is that
one of these critics had said that I have the most
beautiful voice in the world.*

What compelled me to get on the red dot for
TEDxBirmingham was to show others how we
can help each other to understand, how we can
help each other have a voice. After having given
my TEDx talk on using frustration as learning
opportunity to communicate better, I was invited
to assist as a speaker coach for
TEDxYouth@MBJH—and I am still serving as
a speaker coach and finding new ways to help
the youth find their voices.

When I became an active member of the Junior
League of Birmingham (JLB) the following
year, I was asked (by Casey Gamble) to serve as
an ADA compliance consultant as part of my
placement for the Vulcan Park & Museum.
Throughout that year, I conducted surveys and
compiled an inch-thick recommendation report
to share my findings, which resulted in
presentations to help train the staff and

volunteers the importance of inclusive
awareness through communication strategies
with various individuals. This endeavor led to
my being honored as a Spear Hero for the
Vulcans Community Awards 2020, where I
expressed the importance of having a voice and
the hope of my efforts of helping at least one
person that would benefit the community.

I managed the social media for JLB before and
during the pandemic, which honed my creative
communication strategies due to virtual
interactions and mask-wearing regulations.
Through these two years of social media
management, I focused on ensuring that others
experience authentic connection by sharing
essential information to foster strong well-being.
At the same time, I served on the DE&I
taskforce to provide a perspective on what we
could do as an organization. I continued my
active years in publications, with the last and
final issue of *Newsheet* commemorating the
centennial year of the JLB. These active years
have cemented my love for Birmingham because
I pored over artifacts and literature about the
history of the Magic City while gathering
content for the publications and online
networking platforms.

Apart from volunteering, I serve the community
by teaching students the value of communication
through writing and speaking. As an adjunct
professor of English at Jefferson State
Community College since 2017, I encourage

students to express their voices on paper and on screen. I push them to write a lot, and the writing prompts drive my pedagogy, the core of my autoethnographic doctoral dissertation on college teacher development.

Therefore, I am thankful for my family tradition of reading each night. As a Xennial, I grew up without today's technology, which highlighted the importance of eye contact, in-person interactions, and manual information processing. My personal and professional experiences are tightly intertwined in literacy.

Answering the call to help advance literacy education across Central Alabama, I accepted the role as the Director of Development and Communications at The Literacy Council of Central Alabama and its mission to improve the lives of adults and their families through literacy education that teaches people to read, write, and speak English.

And, this role fits neatly into my world, where I get to continue the following passions: teach English Composition at Jeff State, AI grading facilitator for the "Teaching with AI" course offered by the Biggio Center for the Enhancement of Teaching and Learning at Auburn University, content creator for Nomad Tax international accounting firm for digital nomads and American expats, monthly columnist for *Lakeside Living* magazine, Junior League of Birmingham active member, and

Creative Communications Consultant (published poet, Auburn High Class of 1998 class reunion chairperson, editor, educator, ADA compliance consultant, marketing/graphic designer, TEDxYouth@MBJH speaker coach, TEDxBirmingham speaker, and keynote speaker).

Let's not forget that I do Pure Barre and finish half-marathons (#CampbellStrong #RunForRobert).

I keep moving

I keep focused

I keep faith

I believe in serving others as much as I can in
many areas of my little bitty life.

I yearn for others to learn as much as I am
learning.

I desire for others to have insightful hope,
because I do.

And, doing what I can in my calling gives me
more opportunity to uplift others by motivating
them to love reading, writing, and speaking.

...because
each one of us
has a voice
worth hearing...

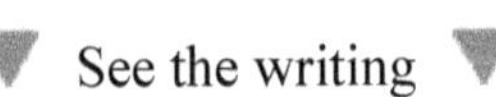
See the writing